This unique interdiscipl...
begins where most studies ...
sivism leave off—with the in...
public policy on the econom...
Wisconsin tax reforms as a to... for political inquiry, the author combines
economic and historical analysis to
demonstrate how and why the state's
model income tax and singularly high
corporate tax actually retarded its economic growth during an era whose very
name signified progress. Students of
public policy, whether they are economists, political scientists, or historians,
will find in the book an examination
of inter-state variations in economic
structure that offers a compelling explanation of the character of progressive reform across the nation.

Based on capital-cost calculations,
the author begins with a detailed comparison of Wisconsin's economy to
that of states with similar resources,
revealing for the first time the devas-
tating effect of the state's early income
taxes. He proceeds to explore the ideology that resulted in a public policy
so far out of step with other tax reforms of the period and relates it to
thus-far neglected elements in the
state's political economy: the political isolation of its manufacturers; the
strength of farm interests who sought
to create an "agricultural service state";
the alliance between farmers and utility
corporations for tax purposes; and the
intellectual failures of the tax experts
who participated in the "Wisconsin
Idea."

Wisconsin's income tax should be seen as more than an irrational means of political manipulation. As Brownlee's study shows, it is also a useful indicator of progressive concepts of democracy within a capitalist, pluralistic society.

PROGRESSIVISM
and
ECONOMIC GROWTH

W. Elliot Brownlee, Jr.

PROGRESSIVISM

and

ECONOMIC GROWTH

The Wisconsin Income Tax
1911—1929

National University Publications
KENNIKAT PRESS • 1974
Port Washington, N.Y. • London

Manufactured in the United States of America

Published by
Kennikat Press Corp.
Port Washington, N.Y./London

Library of Congress Cataloging in Publication Data

Brownlee, W.   Elliot, 1941-
Progressivism and economic growth

(National university publications) (Series in American studies)
Includes bibliographical references.
1. Income tax - - Wisconsin - - History. 2. Wisconsin - - Economic conditions. 3. Progressivism (U.S. politics)
I. Title.
HJ4655.W6B76   336.2'4'09775   74-80065
ISBN 0-8046-9091-X

To Mary Margaret

ACKNOWLEDGMENTS

The greatest debts acquired in writing this book are those to my wife, Mary Margaret Brownlee, for her confidence in the project and the application of her exceptional critical abilities, and to my mentor at the University of Wisconsin, Eric E. Lampard, whose wit and insight supported me during the process of dissertation formulation. Numerous others read the manuscript as well; but most helpful were Morton Borden, Paul W. Glad, Otis L. Graham, Carl V. Harris, Robert Nesbit, and Morton Rothstein.

For their assistance in the tasks of research, I am grateful to the staff of the Wisconsin Department of Taxation and librarians at the State Historical Society of Wisconsin, the Wisconsin State Archives, the Wisconsin Legislative Reference Library, the Butler Library of Columbia University, the Yale University Library, and the libraries of the University of California at Berkeley, Los Angeles, and Santa Barbara. To the University of California, Santa Barbara, and the John Randolph Haynes and Dora Haynes Foundation I am appreciative of a summer fellowship which facilitated completion of a finished manuscript. Melva McClatchey took my very rough draft and produced an expertly typed manuscript.

Finally, I have an obligation to the innumerable historians whose interest in Wisconsin has made that state's past a uniquely rich source for understanding the development of American society.

W. Elliot Brownlee, Jr.

CONTENTS

TABLES

INTRODUCTION:
A PROBLEM IN POLITICAL ECONOMY

Power has always held a fascination for historians of American society, who have proceeded to analyze it within the normative framework of an ostensibly equalitarian society. Perhaps their most difficult problem, in both normative and analytical terms, has been to assess the politics associated with the expansion of government that began in the late nineteenth century. One challenge has been to determine the relative strength of groups contending for the benefits of governmental functions in the regulation of economic life, the provision of public goods and services, and the financing of public activities. Another has been to discern the central thrust of new policy directions, to decide whether governmental expansion represented equalitarian initiatives intended to diffuse social and economic opportunities, reflected the needs of elites seeking to insulate their power in an anti-democratic fashion, or stemmed from a more complex interplay of political interests that conformed only ambiguously to the tenets of an equalitarian society.

The first generation of historians of the emerging welfare state characterized the widening of governmental responsibilities as the expression of lower-class economic interests.[1] A second generation, stimulated by concurrent developments within more rigorous social-science crafts, emphasized either middle-class status problems or competition among class interests as determining the shape of public policy.[2] Most recently, yet another generation has found the expansion of government, particularly at the federal level, to be a response primarily to upper-class concerns, especially those of large units of corporate power, for the stabilization of the economy.[3] This latest interpretive thrust has stood the class interpretation of the first generation on its head and criticized the second generation for failing to give sufficient weight to the power of an emerging corporate elite.

Seldom have historians assessed the economic outcomes of governmental policy in order to investigate the distribution of power. While agreeing, more or less, on the significance of economic stakes to political contests, political historians have tended to place analysis of marketplace conditions in a secondary position. Unfortunately, during the last two decades, economic historians have displayed little sustained interest in the economic effects of government policy with which to aid political historians. Although recent attempts to improve the theoretical and quantitative aspects of economic history have dealt indirectly with the role of government, as in studies of education and the level of government activity, they have not accorded public policy a prominent place in American economic development.[4] "New" economic historians have been attracted by the view that, in the context of a capitalist society, reallocations of resources induced by government rather than the market are apt to be misallocations. Further, they tend to the contrary view that such intervention has played only a minimal role in the economic development of the United States.[5]

Despite this general neglect of economic effects by political and economic historians, the analysis of government activity, including its evaluation as well as the definition of its objectives, can proceed less precariously if the economic consequences are known.[6] This is not to say that it is necessary to know the consequences in order to determine the objectives of policy. But not only do politicians often display an understandable propensity to obscure their real intentions, but also the impact of important sectors of policy extends over many years or even decades, interacting continually with the aspirations and technical capacities of many policy-makers. Consequently, knowledge of the results of public policy must improve the total understanding of institutional change, including the origins and goals of such change.

Taxation, which determines in large part how the costs of government will be allocated among the members of society, is an attractive tool for analyzing the distribution of political power and the related economic impact of governmental policy. For the early decades of the twentieth century, the study of taxation is especially interesting because the period witnessed a dramatic shift in the revenue sources of state and local governments. Income tax revenues partially replaced both the tariff revenues of the federal government and, to a lesser degree, the general property tax revenues of the state and local governments. The portion of general revenues provided by indirect taxes (sales taxes and tariffs) to the federal government fell from almost 75% in 1902 to about 25% by the 1920's. Meanwhile, revenues produced by income taxes accounted for almost 50% of general revenues. (See Table I–1.) On the state and local level, income tax revenues made up about 2% of revenues by the 1920's. Although only a small fraction of all revenues, income taxes were important in allowing property tax revenues to decline from over 67% to about 60% of state and local revenues raised during the late 1920's. (See Table I–2.)

Many historians have concluded that the increasing resort to income taxation was crucial to the expansion of governmental activity during the twentieth century.[7] Those same historians also find a significant and broadly based effort to create a service-regulatory state in the expansion of government since the late nineteenth century. But they often neglect the possibility that the same revenues could have been obtained by means other than the income tax. In particular, tariff reform and sales taxes at the federal level and, at the state and local level, improved systems of property taxation, user charges and fees, and sales taxes might well have been able to produce the same tax revenues. Moreover, greater use of debt financing at all levels would have provided supplementary funds. In

Table I–1.

Composition of General Revenue of Federal Government by Source

	Individ- ual income tax	Corpo- ration income tax	Indirect taxes	Death and gift taxes	Other taxes
1902	—	—	74.58%	0.77%	3.22%
1913	—	—	63.62	—	1.56
1922		45.94%	27.29	3.29	3.36
1927	20.00%		28.64%	24.75	2.05	1.07
1932	15.93		23.52	28.84	1.61	1.42
1936	13.09		14.65	37.46	7.41	3.72
1942	21.67		31.97	23.16	2.85	3.29
1948	43.60		21.86	17.28	2.01	0.80
1954	42.32		30.23	14.85	1.34	0.67

SOURCE: U.S. Department of Commerce, Bureau of the Census, *Historical Statistics of the United States, Colonial Times to 1957* (Washington, 1960), pp. 723–24.

Table I–2.

Composition of State and Local Government Revenue, by Source (from State and Local Sources)

	Individ- ual income tax	Corpo- ration income tax	Sales and gross receipts tax	Property tax	Other taxes	Charges and miscel- laneous general revenue
1902	—	—	2.69%	67.82%	12.10%	11.43%
1913	—	—	2.29	66.01	10.85	14.42
1922	0.85%	1.15%	3.04	65.62	8.69	12.98
1927	.91	1.19	6.09	61.25	9.39	13.83
1932	.97	1.03	9.82	58.62	10.08	11.38
1936	1.82	1.34	17.64	48.66	10.20	8.87
1942	2.25	2.21	19.13	36.92	8.89	8.39
1948	2.75	3.00	22.49	31.01	8.29	10.36
1954	3.48	2.40	22.44	30.74	9.00	12.27

SOURCE: Bureau of the Census, *Historical Statistics,* p. 726.

judging the magnitude of alternative revenue sources, one should note the improvements in property taxation that have enabled it not only to survive but also to remain a buoyant source of revenues. Furthermore, the share of federal revenues generated by indirect taxes did not decline between 1927 and 1936; even during the New Deal, the federal use of income tax revenues actually declined, in relative terms. In short, the adoption of income taxation may not in itself evidence a movement toward the modern service-regulatory state.

The adoption of income taxation may represent public policy endeavors in fact unrelated to the creation of the service-regulatory state. It has been suggested that the adoption of income taxation had nothing to do with government's need for greater resources but was an expression of the principle of taxing according to the "ability to pay."[8] A closely related view claims that government has had to concern itself, through taxation, with the distribution of economies and diseconomies external to the cost and income calculation provided by the market.[9] Thus, by changing tax structures, governments have sought to bring about internalization of external diseconomies by business firms, rather than merely to raise revenues for financing services and regulation.[10] Other historians have spoken of income taxation primarily as a victory of democracy. With that framework, some have emphasized the intent to destroy large combinations of wealth and related concentrations of power.[11] However, it is possible, as one historian has pointed out, that the proponents even of graduated income taxes sought only to redistribute the costs of government and had no desire to reduce the concentration of capital.[12]

Historians have identified the two fundamental objectives of taxation—to raise revenues and to bring about a redistribution of income and wealth; however, they have left the thrust of income taxation ambiguous. Further inquiry is essential to clarify the central purpose of tax policy, especially in the initial years of the income tax. Such study should sharpen our insights into the redirection of government, especially as to whether progressive politicians were interested in building a modern state addressed to the problems of industrial society or were more absorbed with redistributing income to meet the demands of the politically powerful.

Within the changing contours of national taxation, the experience of Wisconsin during the progressive era is of considerable analytic value. Wisconsin contributed the first comprehensive and effectively administered income tax, served as a model for other states and the federal government in the search for tax systems more appropriate to a maturing industrial order, and, until the Great Depression, provided the only example of a system of state income taxation that relied heavily on the taxation of corporate profits.[13] Thus, the state's institutional history promises to be a rich source for the assessment of both the direction of tax reform, particularly the adoption of income taxation, and the character of the progressive state.

The Wisconsin experience becomes even more intriguing because of the controversy over the sources and direction of public activities associated with Wisconsin progressivism. Discussion of Wisconsin progressivism parallels the general discussion of progressivism and affords a long menu of descriptions. One can believe that the Wisconsin progressives were representatives of a latter-day Populist movement intent on redistributing wealth toward farmers,[14] or the initiators of a service-regulatory state to meet the needs of farmers as small businessmen in an industrial society,[15] or the elitist engineers of a set of institutional reforms confirming the preeminent economic power of the large corporations,[16] or the movers of a highly diverse urban reform effort designed to civilize economic competition and provide the basis for the efficient management of industrial society.[17] Although the last interpretation has the widest support among historians, the fundamental issues appear unresolved. At the very least, a clear concept of the nature of tax policy during the period can assist in refining competing interpretations of Wisconsin progressivism.[18]

This study of Wisconsin's political economy between 1900 and 1930 begins where the study of progressivism has tended to leave off—with the impact of public policy on the economy.[19] It begins with the presumption that one should be in a better position to assess the direction of both Wisconsin tax reform and the progressive politics that reform represents after analyzing the long-term economic effects of that reform. The effects singled out for special attention here are those associated with the processes of economic growth. Although the subject of economic growth is significant on its own merits, in the context of this study it also provides a focus for a political inquiry. The prevailing assumption on behalf of progressivism is that Wisconsin's income tax did not inhibit economic growth and, more generally, that the full-scale liberal welfare state has been consistent with the nation's maximization of growth opportunities. Such a judgment is not simply one made by historians; it was a very central assumption of the Wisconsin progressives. However, the most significant opponents of Wisconsin income taxation, the state's largest domestic manufacturers, dissented. By providing a test of the manufacturers' hypothesis that the income tax in Wisconsin did, in fact, retard economic growth, this study also provides evidence for evaluating the popular contention that Wisconsin progressivism represented a very broadly based response to the social problems posed by industrialization. This study reconsiders that familiar characterization in the light of new economic information.

Finally, the study explains the redirection of tax policy in terms of the distribution of political power, with particular reference to the relative role of business, through its scrutiny of the intimate set of relationships linking the pace of economic growth in Wisconsin, the characteristics of the Wisconsin tax system, and the political substance of Wisconsin progressivism.

1

TAXATION AND CAPITAL FORMATION

I

Beginning in the 1920's public finance studies attempted to confront the problem of determining the impact of state and local tax systems on economic development. Evolving from this continuing inquiry has been a predominant view that minimizes the detrimental influence of those taxes on economic growth. This "consensus" position is based on a poorly specified theoretical foundation and, in the case of Wisconsin's experience between 1900 and 1930, is contradicted by an alternative approach founded on firmer theoretical underpinnings.

Virtually all studies that have sought to measure the effect of state and local tax burdens on industrial activity have failed to consider adequately how taxes bear upon economic growth. Using the most comprehensive and productive investigations as examples, one finds basically only simple correlations taken between industrial performance and tax burden (defined, variously, as the ratio of state and local taxes to operating costs, sales, or value added) over the states, primarily for the period since World War II. This method has revealed little or no evidence to link tax differentials with interstate differences in industrial growth. But the measures applied to tax burden fre-

quently have been ambiguous. Moreover, the search for correlations generally omits the specification of a process by
which tax policy might adversely affect growth. Hence these
studies cannot discount the influence of taxation. [1] Definition
of the manner in which taxes affect economic growth is also
neglected in the studies that compare tax loads on individual
firms (including hypothetical firms among various locations),
in those which weigh taxes as a locational factor, and in those
which compare interstate differences in tax "costs" with differentials of other costs.[2]

In contrast to earlier approaches, testing focused on capital formation permits consideration of the effect of taxes on
regional aggregate growth without neglecting the process by
which taxes affected growth.[3] More specifically, we should test
the hypothesis that Wisconsin's tax structure retarded capital
formation within the corporate-manufacturing sector during
the period 1911-1929. In analyzing the influence of taxation on
capital formation and economic growth in Wisconsin, it is
profitable to concentrate on the behavior of manufacturing
corporations rather than to study corporations in general. For
one thing, the manufacturers were the main carriers of the corporate income tax load; their taxable income accounted for
over two thirds of all taxable income earned by corporations
doing business in Wisconsin. (See Table 1–A.) For another,

Table 1–A.
Taxable Income of Corporations Doing Business in Wisconsin

Years (available)	Manufacturing corporations ($)	All corporations ($)	Share of manufacturing corporations
1913	33,030,596	52,191,412	66.54%
1916	48,065,064	69,828,852	71.59
1919	96,760,316	134,191,896	72.11
1922	87,635,942	129,256,551	67.80
1924	87,190,358	124,120,605	70.26
1925	119,712,028	169,122,061	70.80
1927*	113,468,790	168,728,490	67.25

*Average for 1926-28.

SOURCE: State of Wisconsin, Tax Commission, *Report, 1914,*
p. 213; *1918,* p. 109; *1920,* p. 64; *1924,* p. 35; *1928,* p. 83; *1930,* pp.
250–253.

the prosperity of the manufacturing sector was closely associated with income growth in the Great Lakes states between
1909 and 1929.[4]

II

The question of the effect of direct taxation on capital
formation turns on the nature of investment behavior and
competitive conditions. Analysis of that impact is no better
than one's investment theory. The Wisconsin defenders of income taxation lacked a clearly defined investment theory; but
as they generally believed that businessmen maximized profits,
they consequently held that businessmen had used up their
market power before the tax on the returns to capital was
imposed. Hence, in reaction to an income tax, businessmen
could not make any short-run adjustments in production and
employment, with the result that the tax reduced profits in the
state. Assuming that the flow of capital responds to profits or
to the rate of return leads to the conclusion that a state income
tax, with other conditions unchanged, would reduce the flow
of capital into the state and retard capital formation. (More
generally put, a tax on capital that did not apply uniformly to
all sectors of the economy would reduce the flow of capital
into the sector or sectors that were taxed.[5])

The theory of investment behavior held by the proponents
of income taxation in Wisconsin conforms with the body of
theory that has had considerable success in explaining investment behavior since World War II.[6] This description of investment behavior views investment as responsive to the value,
discounted to the present, of all income anticipated as flowing
from that investment. This "present value" of all expected future income is defined as "net worth"; under this investment
theory, the demand for capital stock is determined in such a
way as to maximize "net worth." In contrast to descriptions of
investment that would admit the shifting of income taxes to
other parties through adjustments in production, wages, and
prices, this theory specifies perfect competition or competition

in which all firms accept market prices, as well as profit-maximization.[7] Demand for capital stock, in this theory, responds primarily to what is known as the user cost of capital, or the real economic costs of capital to those using capital, regardless of whether or not they own the capital they use. User cost of capital in turn can be defined, under conditions in which firms maximize profits, in terms of a set of variables that are independent of each other. These include the price of capital goods, the rate of depreciation of capital goods, the rate of interest charged on capital, the rate of income taxation, the rate of property taxation, and variables that take into account how government allows firms to deduct depreciation, interest, capital losses, and property taxes in calculating their taxable income. In short, this real economic cost of capital reveals the amount users of capital should charge themselves in order to maximize their profits.[8]

Without further historical investigation into the nature of investment functions, we cannot say with complete certainty that firms maximized profits according to the assumptions just discussed. But, given the strong, mounting evidence that business has exhibited such behavior over the past 25 years and the very serious weaknesses inherent in specifying alternative investment theories, our particular choice of a theory of investment is the most reasonable one possible.[9] Furthermore, even the defenders of the income tax, both experts and politicians, argued that the manufacturers themselves would pay the income tax and not be able to pass it on through manipulation of production, prices, and wages.[10] Hence, our assumptions in fact lend a decidedly conservative cast to our test.

Using the definition of capital costs just described, we can construct an estimate of the costs of capital resulting from state and local direct taxation. Such an estimate can be made with direct and indirect data on income, taxes, and capital investment. Further, the calculation of capital costs can be performed for various industries and for the entire manufacturing sector in both Wisconsin and competitor states. If taxes resulted in a cost of capital that was higher in Wisconsin than in competing states, we would conclude that the demand for capital goods was lower in Wisconsin, that investment was lower in Wisconsin, and that Wisconsin taxes exerted an in-hibiting influence on capital formation. Also, the relative cost of capital for Wisconsin can be calculated for benchmark years to form a picture of the trends in the state's relative tax burden. To summarize, the concept of the cost of capital provides us with a test of Wisconsin's relative tax burden, construed in terms of capital formation.

III

Before turning to the results of the capital-costs test, we should mention one assumption already made implicitly. That assumption is that the income tax did not bring about a larger social overhead investment and services that would permit a more efficient use of capital in Wisconsin than in the region as a whole. However, it is necessary to consider the possibility that a higher level of government activity in Wisconsin gave manufacturers a competitive edge over those in other states, despite significantly higher costs of capital. It is necessary to ask if the income tax generated revenues for expanded social overhead investment and services that resulted in economies of scale, reduced transaction costs, or diminished risks. Such gains, in turn, might have permitted a more efficient use of capital and compensated for higher capital costs.

Several considerations, however, tend to discount such expenditure effects. For one thing, data on per capita costs of government indicate that Wisconsin made no significant depar-ture from the pattern of the region. In fact, by 1928, Michigan, Indiana, and Illinois all surpassed Wisconsin in per capita tax collections, despite the fact that, at the same time, Wisconsin's per capita debt was lower than that of any other state in the region and was becoming relatively smaller. Thus, per capita governmental expenditures were actually lower than in Michi-gan, Indiana, and Illinois. Wisconsin's income tax may have allowed the state to avoid a significantly larger debt obligation, but it did not enlarge the relative size of public expenditures.[11]

In addition, the sizeable flow of income tax revenues to northern Wisconsin during the 1920's strongly suggests that the use of such revenues inhibited economic growth by bringing about a misallocation of resources. To the extent that this misallocation occurred, focusing on capital costs understates the retarding influence of Wisconsin's income tax. Further, the character of public expenditures in Wisconsin shifted over the period toward the support of the agricultural service-state, toward the financing of services that benefitted most directly the interests of specialized agriculture. The manufacturers in effect found themselves compelled to purchase services on behalf of the agricultural sector.[12] Thus, the neglect of the revenue effects of taxation in the economic analysis tends to understate the detrimental impact of the Wisconsin tax system on economic growth.

IV

To perform the capital-costs test, we made estimates of the cost of capital in three benchmark years (1909, 1919, and 1929) for Wisconsin and the other Great Lakes states. The estimating procedures used tend to guarantee a conservative test; any error is most likely to be in the direction of relative lower capital costs for manufacturing in Wisconsin.[13] Perhaps the most significant way in which the impact of the Wisconsin income tax is understated results from the use of "current" values for tax-structure parameters, rather than expected or anticipated values As it is impossible to know, of course, what levels of taxation firms expected in the future, one is forced to rely on "current" observable quantities. Nonetheless, manufacturers, until the late 1920's, tended to be highly pessimistic about the future course of Wisconsin tax experiments and may well have adjusted investment plans accordingly, thus reacting even more negatively than the capital-costs test would indicate.[14]

The estimates of capital costs reveal that the rate in

Wisconsin for all industries was slightly greater than that in the Great Lakes states in 1909 and somewhat larger in 1919. (See Table 1–B.) In 1909, the industry-wide cost of capital in Wisconsin exceeded that within any Great Lakes state, with the exception of Michigan. In 1919, the cost of capital in Indiana also surpassed that in Wisconsin, but Wisconsin's rate was considerably higher than that of Ohio or Illinois. If one accepts the less reliable 1929 estimates, there was a relative decline in the rates of Indiana and Wisconsin but a sharp increase in those of Illinois that left the cost of capital somewhat lower in Wisconsin than in the region as a whole but still larger than that in either Ohio or Indiana.[15]

Table 1–B.
Real Cost of Capital in Manufacturing for Great Lakes States

Industry group and state[a]	1909	1919	1929
All industry:			
Illinois	.09407	.19290	.20293
Indiana	.09753	.35037	.18897
Michigan	.10677	.37489	.19808
Ohio	.09646	.21274	.18533
Wisconsin	.10541	.30379	.19171
All Great Lakes	.09800	.25672	.19242
1. Food products:			
Illinois	.11281	.23201	.17894
Indiana	.11525	.25800	.19854
Michigan	.11270	.31935	.22065
Ohio	.09258	.25827	.19464
Wisconsin	.11215	.28635	.18301
All Great Lakes	.11333	.25582	.18921
2. Textiles:			
Illinois	.08912	.18174	.26246
Indiana	.09265	.25080	.41811
Michigan	.09790	.24689	.64203
Ohio	.09110	.18691	.52717
Wisconsin	.08837	.29827	.37025
All Great Lakes	.09095	.18836	.35789
3. Leather:			
Illinois	.09321	.21738	.20638
Indiana	.09780	.18174	.38118
Michigan	.10343	.49916	.26495
Ohio	.09957	.21963	.24452
Wisconsin	.10037	.49079	.16562
All Great Lakes	.09890	.33713	.21126
4. Rubber:			
Illinois	.09128	.18592	.31006
Indiana	.09626	.28327	.23271
Michigan	.08556	.44608	.48916

Table 1–B. (Continued)

Industry group and state[a]	1909	1919	1929
Ohio	.09814	.18592	.16985
Wisconsin	.08556	.40528	.18686
All Great Lakes	.09792	.25458	.18193
5. Lumber and wood:			
Illinois	.09212	.23734	.24338
Indiana	.09553	.22698	.16327
Michigan	.11125	.22080	.16834
Ohio	.09555	.22003	.19691
Wisconsin	.11187	.26900	.15831
All Great Lakes	.10379	.20769	.17871
6. Paper and pulp:			
Illinois	.08520	.24916	.22367
Indiana	.08213	.23688	.15803
Michigan	.09369	.27903	.16516
Ohio	.09592	.25592	.17298
Wisconsin	.09031	.28702	.14865
All Great Lakes	.09085	.24966	.16334
7. Printing and publishing:			
Illinois	.10120	.27258	.19347
Indiana	.10404	.27913	.22500
Michigan	.10494	.34038	.22033
Ohio	.10338	.30291	.20052
Wisconsin	.10277	.29985	.21453
All Great Lakes	.10255	.28755	.20249
8. Chemicals:			
Illinois	.07271	.14367	.22766
Indiana	.07074	.22930	.27971
Michigan	.07949	.26247	.22737
Ohio	.07888	.14367	.24733
Wisconsin	.08058	.19684	.41081
All Great Lakes	.07701	.14367	.24142
9. Stone, clay, and glass:			
Illinois	.08600	.20615	.16566
Indiana	.08985	.20135	.14886
Michigan	.10145	.22026	.15951
Ohio	.08783	.21978	.15127
Wisconsin	.08778	.41019	.28039
All Great Lakes	.08928	.22821	.15802
10. Metals:			
Illinois	.08792	.17585	.20302
Indiana	.08832	.29907	.18869
Michigan	.09055	.39170	.19544
Ohio	.08986	.17585	.18346
Wisconsin	.08810	.30021	.18771
All Great Lakes	.08900	.23980	.19016

[a]No separate estimation was made for the "miscellaneous" industries included in the "all industry" total.

SOURCE: See Appendix.

Industry-group variations within the general pattern indicate a less favorable situation for Wisconsin than does the all-industry summary. In some industries (food, rubber, paper and pulp, stone, clay, and glass, and metals), capital costs in Wisconsin were lower than the regional level in 1909. But by 1919 the state's real cost of capital exceeded the Great Lakes average in every industry category. In 1929, her capital costs were higher in the textile, rubber, printing and publishing, chemicals, and stone, clay, and glass industrial groups.

The general weakening of Wisconsin's competitive costs position between 1909 and 1919 was the most important trend. (Table 1–C displays the ratio of cost of capital in Wisconsin to that in Wisconsin's region.) For all industries, capital costs were eight points higher than in the Great Lakes states as a whole in 1909, but by 1919 they were 18 points higher in Wisconsin. By 1929, capital costs declined, equalling the Great Lakes average. However, the likelihood of the convergence of Wisconsin and her region, given the weaker estimates for 1929, is smaller than for the divergence between 1909 and 1919. Also, the 1929 estimates are somewhat questionable in that the marked changes in taxation enacted in 1925, increasing the tax payments of manufacturers, are not readily apparent from the 1929 data. Consequently, if there was a reversal of Wisconsin's relative capital-costs position during the 1920's, on the scale the test indicates, it almost certainly occurred in the waning years of the decade.[16]

Table 1–C.
Ratio of Real Capital Costs in Wisconsin
to Great Lakes Average
(100 = Great Lakes average)

Industry group	1909	1919	1929
All industry	108	118	100
1. Food products	99	112	97
2. Textiles	101	158	104
3. Leather	101	146	78
4. Rubber	87	159	103
5. Lumber and wood	108	130	89
6. Paper and pulp	99	115	91
7. Printing and publishing	100	104	106
8. Chemicals	105	137	170
9. Stone, clay, and glass	98	180	177
10. Metals	99	125	99

SOURCE: Table 1–B.

The divergence between 1909 and 1919 holds for every industry group. The cost of capital in the food industry, for instance, rose from below that in the Great Lakes states to almost 12 points above the regional average. In the lumber industry, the real cost of capital increased from 8 points to 30 points above the regional average. In the paper and pulp industry, capital costs in Wisconsin were slightly less than the regional level in 1909, but by 1919 they were 15 points above that for the Great Lakes states as a whole. Beginning from a level slightly below that for the region, the real cost of capital in the Wisconsin stone, clay, and glass industry increased to 80 points above the regional average in 1919. From a similar base in 1909, the relative cost of capital in Wisconsin's metal industry increased to more than 25 points above the level for the metal industry in the region. The corresponding increase in the chemical industry was from 5 points to 37 points above the regional level. Without detailing the trends, the decline in Wisconsin's relative position between 1919 and 1929 found for the aggregate of all industries also held true for every industry group, except for printing and publishing, chemicals, and stone, clay, and glass.

Under our formulation of capital costs, the interstate variations in taxation account for all interstate differentials. To isolate the income tax effect, we can recalculate capital costs for the situation that would have prevailed if Wisconsin governments had levied no income tax in 1919 and 1929 and all other conditions had remained unchanged. Hypothetical Wisconsin capital costs can then be compared with the corresponding capital costs for the entire Great Lakes region. (See Table 1–D.)

This comparison indicates that if Wisconsin had eliminated the corporate income tax, capital costs in each industry category would have been two to four points lower, relative to the average for all the Great Lakes states.[17] It is clear that eliminating income taxes would have helped correct the state's unfavorable tax situation in 1919. It is worth bearing in mind that the 1919 capital-cost estimate excluded the high wartime income surtaxes, which were added to the "normal" income tax and doubled the effective rate in one year, and made no accounting of the likelihood that manufacturers expected income taxes to increase even more, given the intensive discussion of increasing reliance on the income tax during and after

Table 1–D.
Ratio of Real Capital Costs in Wisconsin
to Great Lakes Average Without Income Taxation
(100 = Great Lakes average)

Industry group	1919	1929
All industry	116	98
1. Food products	110	95
2. Textiles	156	102
3. Leather	144	77
4. Rubber	157	101
5. Lumber and wood	127	86
6. Paper and pulp	113	89
7. Printing and publishing	102	91
8. Chemicals	133	169
9. Stone, clay, and glass	177	175
10. Metals	123	97

World War I.[18] By 1929, the removal of the corporate income tax would have meant relatively a great deal more than in 1919. In most industrial categories, capital costs would have moved to a position either much closer to or substantially lower than the regional average. For all industries, capital costs would have become two points lower than the regional level and, for the crucial metals industry, capital costs would have moved three points below the regional level. In short, throughout our period, income taxation exerted strong upward pressure on the relative level of capital costs in Wisconsin.

V

The implication and significance of the test revealing the increase in the cost of capital in Wisconsin, compared with other states in the region, is clear. The relative increase in capital costs resulting from taxation should have inhibited the rate of capital formation in Wisconsin as compared with other states in the state's region. Levels of capital formation in Wisconsin and the region should have diverged just as capital costs did. As a result of the higher costs of capital, the desired levels of investment and net additions to capital stock should have been relatively lower in Wisconsin than elsewhere in the region.[19] The differential is seen to have been even greater when the cost of capital is compared with that in Illinois, Wisconsin's closest neighbor. Firms having a choice of locating or expanding facilities in either Illinois or Wisconsin would, on the basis of capital costs, easily choose Illinois. The divergence in capital costs between Wisconsin and the Great Lakes states between 1909 and 1919 was of a very dramatic magnitude, and the detrimental impact of this trend for capital formation may well have far outweighed any later reversal.[20]

The competitive situation with regard to capital costs had possibly improved by 1929, but even so the upward trend occurred only toward the end of our period. Even by 1929, the relative size of capital costs in Wisconsin was not decidedly favorable. In 1929, the real cost of capital was lower in two states of the region and approximately the same in the region as a whole.

The income tax was detrimental, in a significant way, to Wisconsin's capital-costs position. Without corporate income taxation, Wisconsin would have been a more attractive site for investment in the manufacturing sector from 1911 through 1929. Throughout the period, the Wisconsin income tax meant that investors always faced a cost of capital that was higher than it would have been without the tax. Although the absolute magnitude of this differential was not overwhelmingly large at any particular instant, it influenced Great Lakes investment decisions continuously over a period of two decades. However, as capital markets in the Midwest were well-developed by the early twentieth century,[21] this marginal difference in capital costs should have meant a very substantial shift in the flow of investment funds and a significant departure from optimal distribution of capital stock within the Great Lakes states.[22]

VI

Finally, two caveats must be added. First, the capital-costs test in no way reflects upon the character of all income taxes. The user cost of capital, as it has been applied here, is a valuable instrument for the analysis of taxes that bear upon interstate differentials in the cost of capital services, and the capital-costs test does not necessarily question the validity of all state income taxes. Thus, framers of Wisconsin's income tax could have designed an income tax that avoided or reduced the increase in the costs of capital to manufacturers. To have done so, in general terms, they could have exempted manufacturers from the tax, or taxed them at lower statutory or effective rates, or provided the means for manufacturers to obtain compensating reductions in property taxation. Those and other possibilities were the subject of discussion in Wisconsin's income tax debates. Further, federal income taxation poses yet another more attractive way to pursue income taxation. In fact, it is reasonable to submit that an equivalent federal income tax would be far preferable to a state income tax because its imposition of a uniform increase in capital costs would not distort the interstate distribution of capital. On such grounds, it might well be preferable to meet various revenue objectives through federal income taxation (linked, perhaps, with revenue sharing with states and localities) rather than through the use of state and local property taxes.[23]

Second, the capital-costs test provides no evidence that could reflect the environmental costs associated with the process of economic growth but not reckoned by the marketplace. Given the currently spreading persuasion that economic growth has been accompanied by massive environmental externalities resulting from depletion and degradation of natural resources, it might be tempting to surmise that insofar as the Wisconsin tax system retarded economic growth, the Wisconsin progressives moved economic development onto a less costly path for future generations.[24] That possibility evokes two responses. In the first place, governmental action designed to account for environmental costs must be far more complex than simply to retard economic growth and, in fact, may well be most effective within a context of rapidly increasing per capita incomes.[25] In the second place, and more importantly for the assessment of progressivism, at no time did the framers of Wisconsin's tax laws consciously seek for any reason, including environmental protection, to restrict the growth of manufacturing activity.[26]

2

THE IMPACT ON WISCONSIN GROWTH

I

The results of capital-costs test should not lead to the conclusion that Wisconsin taxation halted the industrial development of the state. Certain comparative advantages, favorable labor-market conditions, and the commitment of well-established manufacturers, particularly in the paper and metals industries, insured continued industrial growth in Wisconsin. But as a result of imposing high capital costs through taxation, Wisconsin may well have impeded the course of industrialization and, in turn, economic growth, which was based during our period on the shift of resources from less-productive agricultural enterprise to more-productive manufacturing activity.

The centrality of the process of capital formation to the expansion of manufacturing, the growth of national product, and gains in labor productivity requires careful attention to the level of capital costs. The post-Civil War pace of manufacturing growth, economic expansion, and productivity increases was associated with a constellation of closely bound factors, with the rate of capital formation playing the most central role. The expansion of the stock of capital may well have accounted for most of the growth of national product during our period and most certainly permitted the sustained substitution of capital for labor that produced substantial advances in the productivity of labor.[1] Moreover, the refinement of capital markets by the beginning of this period had promoted and had become necessary to the diffusion of high-productivity enterprise to the Great Lakes region.[2]

The establishment of an exact quantitative relationship between capital costs and the growth of manufacturing is, however, impossible; we lack a completely articulated model of the economy, including regional components, covering the period. Nonetheless, we can suggest the dimensions of taxation's role within an examination of the development of manufacturing activity in the Great Lakes states between 1890 and 1930.

II

A considerable spatial redistribution of manufacturing activity took place within the United States between the end of the Civil War and the conclusion of World War II. The spatial redistribution brought greater industrial specialization by state, although a decreasing specialization by region. This specialization by state meant that the composition and structure of industry varied around the nation and that the concentration of industry depended on factors other than the concentration of population and income. The distribution of raw materials, variations in transportation costs for inputs and outputs, interstate and regional differences in costs of the factors of production, and the variety of levels of government services and costs of government accounted, in an important way, for interstate differences in industrial characteristics.

The Great Lakes states gained the most from this redistribution of manufacturing activity. Between 1869 and 1947, the five states in this region (Ohio, Indiana, Illinois, Michigan, and Wisconsin) increased their share of total value added by manufacturing by 13 percentage points and accounted for over 40% of the absolute increases realized by all the "gaining" states. But the relative advance of the region was not uniform. During the 20-year period from 1889 to 1909, their share of the total gain in manufacturing activity fell drastically, from the 55%

achieved in the preceding two decades to about 20%. The period of greatest relative growth for the Great Lakes region came in the next period, between 1909 and 1929, when the five states produced 60% of the nation's gain in value added by manufacturing production. Thereafter, their pattern of growth was closer to the sluggish 1889–1909 period.[3]

It was during this crucial period of relatively rapid growth for the Great Lakes region that Wisconsin's tax policies brought about sharply increased capital costs and substantially reduced levels of capital formation. As a result of that conjunction of high capital costs and large growth potential, the probability is strong that Wisconsin's competitive disadvantage had very serious ramifications in terms of economic growth. Corroborating this judgment is the clear importance of factors other than market access, such as taxation, in explaining interstate differences in industrial location, especially within regions. Moreover, because the period between 1909 and 1929 was so important for the total growth of the Great Lakes states in the twentieth century, one can reasonably surmise that a more favorable tax policy after 1929 could not have compensated for the earlier disadvantage.

Indeed, the relative strength of Wisconsin's manufacturing sector within the Great Lakes did suffer during the second and third decades of this century. The growth of the manufacturing sector was strong in both Wisconsin and the Great Lakes between 1890 and 1910. (See Table 2-A.) Employment in manufacturing increased from 24% to 31% of the Wisconsin labor force during those two decades. Thus, the relative size of the manufacturing sector, in terms of total employment, increased at a rate of 29%, which was not far from the 32% increase for the region as a whole. But during the next twenty years, the trend was much different. Wisconsin's 72% increase in total manufacturing employment was strong, but it fell short of the 96% increase enjoyed by the region as a whole. (See Table 2-B.) As a result, Wisconsin's rate of increase in manufacturing's relative share was much slower, only about 3%, as contrasted with about 9% for all the Lakes states. (See Table

2-A.) A similar pattern emerges from data on value added by manufacturing. (See Table 2-C.) The Great Lakes states accounted for about 24% of the value added by manufacturing in the United States in 1889 and increased their share moderately, at a rate of about 10%, over the next 20 years. At the same time, Wisconsin's share increased even faster, or at a rate of about 12%. But during the following two decades, Wisconsin's performance was much less favorable. Value added by manufacturing grew well over four and one-half times in the Lakes states, as contrasted with a rate well under four times for Wisconsin. (see Table 2-B) In terms of the rate of increase, Wisconsin's share of value added for the entire United States was only 4%, despite the 24% rate for all the Great Lakes states. (see Table 2-C)

A key to the growth of the Great Lakes region between 1910 and 1929 was the expansion of the metals industries, including iron and steel products, nonferrous metals and their products, machinery (including machine tools), and transportation equipment. These industries as a group accounted for 48% of the region's growth in terms of employment and value added by manufacturing during the second and third decades of the century. (see Table 2-D) During these years, the concentration of industries increased until the region accounted for 42% of the United States' employment in 1929, compared with 37% in 1909. Also, it contributed 38% of the value added in all the states, compared with 35% in 1909. (see Table 2-E)

Wisconsin, however, did not participate in the great growth of the metals industries as extensively as her Great Lakes neighbors. Wisconsin's share of labor employed in the metals industries of the Lake area fell from about nine to six per cent between 1909 and 1929, paralleled by an almost identical decline in value added. The greatest contributor to this relative decline was the machinery industry, including the fabrication of machine tools. At the same time Wisconsin suffered sharp declines in shares of employment and value added in the machinery industry, the state's production of metals and metal products lost but little ground and its production of transportation equipment increased.[4] However, the relatively favorable experience of Wisconsin in attracting those particular metals industries was far more than offset by the failure to foster the growth of the machinery producers who constituted the largest metals industry in the Great Lakes states in both 1909 and 1929.

(Tables 2–A through 2–E follow)

Table 2–A.
Manufacturing Employment as a Percentage of
Total Employment for Wisconsin and Great Lakes States

Year	Wisconsin	Great Lakes states
1890	24.35%	25.04%
1900	26.25	27.28
1910	31.32	33.19
1920	34.25	37.36
1930	32.27	35.72
1910/1890	1.29	1.32
1930/1910	1.03	1.09

SOURCE: Harvey S. Perloff *et al., Regions, Resources and Economic Growth* (Baltimore, 1960), pp. 144, 174, 266, 632.

Table 2–B.
Employment and Value Added in Manufacturing Sector
for Wisconsin and Great Lakes States

	Employment		
	1909	1929	1929/1909
Wisconsin	182,583	313,139	1.72
Great Lakes	1,513,764	2,974,216	1.96

	Value added ($)		
	1909	1929	1929/1909
Wisconsin	243,948,955	949,841,682	3.89
Great Lakes	2,177,230,169	9,973,490,317	4.58

SOURCE: U.S. Dept. of Commerce, Bureau of the Census, *Thirteenth Census of the United States, Manufactures, 1909*, VIII, 57; *Fifteenth Census of the United States, Manufactures, 1929*, III, 18.

Table 2–C.
Shares of Value Added by Manufacturing for
Wisconsin and Great Lakes States

	1889	1909	1929	1909/1889	1929/1909
Wisconsin	2.57%	2.88%	3.01%	1.12	1.04
Great Lakes	24.35	25.60	31.64	1.10	1.24
U.S.	100	100	100	1.00	1.00

SOURCE: Richard A. Easterlin, "Redistribution of Manufacturing," p. 125.

Table 2–D.
Importance of Metals Industries to Growth
of Great Lakes Industries, 1909–1928

Industry	Net increase in labor force	Net increase in value added ($)
Metals	706,595	3,744,971,778
All	1,460,452	7,796,260,148
Metals/All	.484	.480

SOURCE: Table 2–B and Table 2–E.

Table 2–E.
Employment and Value Added
in the Metals Industry*

	Employment		Value added ($)	
	1909	1929	1909	1929
All metals:				
Wisconsin	61,156	86,399	69,524,879	293,764,480
Great Lakes	664,746	1,371,341	758,432,119	4,503,403,897
U.S.	1,781,140	3,268,403	2,186,465,726	11,841,303,438
Wisconsin/G.L.	.092	.063	.092	.065
G.L./U.S.	.373	.420	.347	.380
Iron and steel products:				
Wisconsin	5,832	16,749	6,031,979	49,988,071
Great Lakes	120,992	374,223	163,915,126	1,352,733,322
U.S.	310,077	880,882	404,648,467	3,275,054,572
Wis./G.L.	.048	.045	.037	.037
G.L./U.S.	.390	.425	.405	.413
Non-ferrous metals and products:				
Wisconsin	6,341	9,183	5,264,358	24,769,233
Great Lakes	58,376	101,501	58,130,977	306,089,174
U.S.	248,785	314,741	347,236,668	1,131,613,519
Wis./G.L.	.109	.090	.091	.081
G.L./U.S.	.235	.322	.167	.270
Machinery (excluding transportation equipment):				
Wisconsin	34,074	22,158	41,449,452	80,466,361
Great Lakes	286,830	508,945	338,282,595	1,759,431,231
U.S.	714,967	1,091,269	956,372,000	4,349,000,761
Wis./G.L.	.119	.044	.123	.046
G.L./U.S.	.401	.467	.354	.405
Transportation equipment:				
Wisconsin	14,909	38,309	16,779,090	138,540,815
Great Lakes	198,548	386,675	198,103,421	1,085,150,170
U.S.	507,311	981,511	478,208,591	3,085,634,586
Wis./G.L.	.075	.099	.085	.128
G.L./U.S.	.391	.394	.414	.352

*1929 categories were used to classify 1909 industries.

SOURCE: *Thirteenth Census, Manufactures,* VIII, 53, 507–17; IX, 292–95, 328–331, 578–581, 984–989, 1356–1359; *Fifteenth Census, Manufactures,* III, 37–38, 146–148, 167–168, 255–257, 402–406, 566–567.

Thus, while the highly productive metals industries were at the center of the great manufacturing gains in the Great Lakes states in the two decades following the adoption of corporate income taxation, Wisconsin became more specialized in the smaller-scale, less-productive, and lower-wage industries, such as agricultural processing and lumber. That the machinery industry of Wisconsin displayed sluggish growth in this period corroborates the conclusion that relatively heavy taxation of machinery manufacturers very likely retarded that industry in Wisconsin. Such retardation is precisely what would be expected to follow from the thrust of tax policies, particularly for an industry that was highly capital-intensive or relied to an unusual extent on capital goods for its expansion.

After 1911 there was a shift in the pattern of manufacturing in Wisconsin away from specialization in the growth industries of the maturing industrial revolution toward more traditional activities connected with the processing of primary products. As a direct result, levels of labor productivity in manufacturing and average manufacturing wages grew more hesitantly in Wisconsin after 1911 than in the Great Lakes states as a whole. In 1909, the productivity of labor employed in manufacturing in Wisconsin was approximately the same as that in Michigan and Indiana and only slightly less than that in Ohio. (see Table 2-F) By 1929, however, manufacturing labor productivity was lower than in any other state of the region and was reasonably close only to the level of productivity attained in Indiana. In 1909, the average wage level of those employed in manufacturing in Wisconsin had been approximately the same as that for Michigan and Indiana. By 1929, however, Wisconsin's relative wage position had fallen substantially behind that of every state except Indiana.[5]

Table 2–F.
Productivity and Wages in Manufacturing

	Value added per wage earner in manufacturing (as % of U.S. average)	
	1909	1929
Illinois	128%	118%
Indiana	103	101
Michigan	105	107
Ohio	108	108
Wisconsin	105	99
	Wages per wage earner in manufacturing (as % of U.S. average)	
	1909	1929
Illinois	114%	113%
Indiana	98	101
Michigan	100	122
Ohio	107	114
Wisconsin	100	102

SOURCE: Simon Kuznets *et al., Population Redistribution and Economic Growth, United States, 1870–1950, Analyses of Economic Change,* II (Philadelphia, 1960), pp. 128–129.

III

Is it possible to rely only on the capital-costs test in assessing the impact of Wisconsin's revenue system on economic growth, assuming that other industrial location factors had no bearing on the *relative* performance of Wisconsin? That assumption may well be justified, particularly in the light of the centrality of capital formation to growth, but to justify it fully one must examine the force of other locational factors.

One such factor is the relative level of public services available that might provide manufacturers at that location a competitive advantage over manufacturers in other locations. The thrust of evidence here is toward the finding that, if anything, Wisconsin provided a lower level of services to manufacturers than did competing states. Thus the assumption that expenditure effects were uniform among the states very probably tends to underestimate the detrimental force of Wisconsin's total public policy.[6] Ingoring revenue lends the conclusion reached on the basis of the capital costs a distinctly modest cast.

Apart from the rental price of capital, the primary factors

influencing industrial location were the cost of raw materials and the cost of transportation. It is conceivable that these factors also contributed to Wisconsin's economic lethargy from 1909 to 1929 and would have committed Wisconsin to specialization in low-productivity activity even with more favorable tax policies. Although the manufacturing profile of the Great Lakes region increasingly resembled that of the nation during our period, there was a growing specialization of manufacturing by states within the region. Wisconsin's increasing concentration on agricultural processing, particularly of dairy products, was part of this process of differentiation within regional growth. Did the particular path of specialization followed by Wisconsin simply reflect the relative costs of the factors of production, apart from the influence of taxation on the cost of capital?

To be sure, Wisconsin had problems apart from taxation. The state suffered somewhat from being relatively remote from both the coal fields and the steel mills to the east, thus increasing her raw material costs. However, for one central growth industry, machine tool production, the cost of material transportation was a factor of very little significance in the location of plants.[7] Wisconsin's geographic position on the fringe of the Great Lakes also meant relatively high transport costs to markets in her region and in the eastern states. Nonetheless, this disadvantage was quite probably very small, and Wisconsin found itself in excellent position to reach the buoyant Chicago market with its manufactured goods. Moreover, Wisconsin's labor supply conditions probably counteracted any detrimental factors by attracting high value-added activity, especially within the metals industry. Although Wisconsin was not a "low-wage" state, it had a substantial advantage over neighbor states in its more highly skilled labor force, one better suited to the needs of capital-intensive industry.[8]

While the labor force throughout the Great Lakes states tended to be highly skilled by national standards, the skill level of the urban labor force was significantly higher in Wisconsin than in the other states of the region. No widely ac-

cepted measure of labor skills overcomes completely the
problem of limited historical data. However, a useful measure
is the rate of illiteracy, as literacy, in either English or a
foreign language, indicated some schooling and a rudimentary
knowledge of mathematics.[9] In 1910, the literacy level for
the urban labor force, both native American and foreign born,
was higher in Wisconsin than in any other Great Lakes state.
(See Table 2-G.) Adding to Wisconsin's relative skill advantage, productivity in the growth portions of the metals industries remained higher in Wisconsin than in the Great Lakes
region and, indeed, increased relative to the Great Lakes
average, even though labor productivity for the manufacturing
sector as a whole declined from 1909 to 1929. Thus, in the
manufacture of machinery of all types, labor productivity was
3% higher in Wisconsin than the region in 1909 and 5%
higher by 1929. In the manufacture of transportation equipment of all types (automobiles, most importantly), productivity was 13% higher in Wisconsin in 1909 and increased to
a level 29% higher by 1929.[10] Finally, in competing for highly
productive manufacturing activity through labor-related advantages, Wisconsin offered a labor force that, perhaps because
of its cultural qualities, had a significantly lower turnover
rate.[11]

Table 2–G.
Urban Illiteracy Rates, 1910

	Native-Born	Foreign-Born
Illinois	0.6%	10.2%
Indiana	1.3	11.9
Michigan	0.7	9.6
Ohio	0.8	11.3
Wisconsin	0.4	8.7

SOURCE: U.S. Department of Commerce, Bureau of the Census,
Thirteenth Census of the U.S., 1910, Population, Reports by States,
Vol. II, pp. 479, 545, 927; Vol. III, pp. 397, 1077.

To take an important illustration of Wisconsin's attrac-
tions, between 1913 and 1927, the Bucyrus-Erie Company,
manufacturers of earth-moving equipment, invested $3.24 mil-

lion in their South Milwaukee plant, as contrasted with only $1.10 million at their Evansville, Indiana, facility, although they had begun the latter with the stimulus of a large public subsidy in 1910. The historians of the company explain that in Evansville, "unlike South Milwaukee, there was no large body of old-time employees who took pride in turning out a product that would stand up under adverse field conditions, and who imparted this attitude to new personnel."[12]

The locational decisions of the machine-tool industry provide additional evidence that Wisconsin possessed considerable growth potential because of its labor resources. Next to intensive price competition, the shortage of skilled labor was the primary strategic problem of that industry. Wisconsin offered that industry a skilled population and a location that allowed manufacturers to ship cheaply to the tool users of Illinois and Michigan but was isolated enough to markedly discourage skilled workers from migrating to the flourishing auto industry. If there had not been a strong tax disadvantage, the machine-tool industry clearly would have grown very rapidly in Wisconsin.[13]

In short, Wisconsin's labor-market conditions constituted a sizeable compensation for her transport handicaps. Wisconsin, in fact, had important advantages for the location of new firms and the expansion of old, especially those in the "growth" metals industries of the Great Lakes region. Those advantages, focused on a relatively high-quality labor supply, meant that Wisconsin's fundamental pattern of development was neither inevitable nor beyond the control of Wisconsin's politicians. In fact, Wisconsin had significant assets for the "growth" industries of the Great Lakes states, assets that a favorable tax climate for investment could have reinforced (or avoided neutralizing) to produce a more vibrant manufacturing sector. Those assets resulted in Wisconsin's highly favorable performance within the Great Lakes regional economy during the period from 1899 to 1909 and, with a favorable public policy during the subsequent decades, could have maintained a similar relative degree of economic health.

IV

As Iowa and Minnesota, Wisconsin's immediate neighbors to the west, were not mentioned in the capital-costs test, our conclusions as to the growth impact of Wisconsin taxes may be thought biased in two ways. It is arguable that Wisconsin's locational advantages and disadvantages, apart from taxation, were closer to those of the Eastern Plains states than to her Great Lakes neighbors. As a result, ignoring Minnesota and Iowa may have overstated Wisconsin's tax handicap: Wisconsin might have done very well in competing with her western neighbors, especially in the food-processing industries, but poorly in competing with the other Great Lakes states. Further, it might be that Minnesota and Iowa placed even higher tax burdens on industry than Wisconsin, thus equipping Wisconsin with an important locational advantage.

To answer the first argument, Minnesota and Iowa suffered far more than Wisconsin from their distance from the eastern coal fields and steel mills. In addition, these two states were awkwardly situated to ship to the eastern and the even more important Great Lakes markets. This disadvantage precluded any significant development of metals industries in Minnesota and Iowa and contributed strongly to the lower growth rates of these states during the period. Also, as a result, Wisconsin's manufacturing profile resembled that of the Great Lakes region much more closely than that of the Eastern Plains states.[14] In effect, our comparison of capital costs between Wisconsin and the other Lake states focuses on the "marginal" group of firms who were choosing among the Great Lakes states in making investment decisions. The crucial role of the metals industry in the industrial growth of both the Great Lakes states as a region and Wisconsin alone justifies excluding the states of the eastern Great Plains.

To answer the second argument, a comparison of capital costs in Wisconsin with those in the region composed of Wisconsin, Minnesota, and Iowa reveals that Wisconsin's relative capital-costs position, as a result of state and local taxation, was actually less favorable that that of Iowa and Minnesota. In 1909, capital costs for all industries was three points higher in Wisconsin than in the three-state group, and Wisconsin's level was higher that that in either Minnesota or Iowa. (See Tables 2-H and 2-I.) In the food industry, the rate was slightly lower in Wisconsin than in the other two states in 1909, but even that industry lost its slightly favorable position by 1919. Capital costs for all industries, in fact, became relatively much higher for Wisconsin in 1919, with the spread widening from three to seventeen points. The same pattern held for every industry group. And, although there were some minor variations by industry, Wisconsin's relative position among her neighbors was about the same in 1919. Furthermore, the relative change from 1909 was similar whether one considers the state a part of the Eastern Plains or treats it as part of the Great Lakes region. (Compare Tables 1-C and 2-I.) In short, these comparisons argue that analyzing Wisconsin's development even in the context of the Eastern Plain states does not alter the basic finding of a sharply deteriorating capital-costs position for Wisconsin between 1909 and 1919 and a consequent disability in the interstate competition for capital investment.

Table 2–H.
Real Cost of Capital in Manufacturing
for Iowa-Minnesota-Wisconsin

Industry group and state[a]	1909	1919	1929
All industry:			
Iowa	.09463	.26786	.24779
Minnesota	.09879	.18579	.22472
Wisconsin	.10541	.30379	.19171
Total	.10191	.26022	.20771
1. Food products:			
Iowa	.11263	.28285	.18245
Minnesota	.11802	.21810	.17284
Wisconsin	.11215	.28635	.18301
Total	.11396	.25917	.17713
2. Textiles:			
Iowa	.09370	.18174	3.09664
Minnesota	.08447	.18174	.70184
Wisconsin	.09166	.29827	.37025
Total	.09237	.25737	.55602

Table 2-H (Continued)

Industry group and state[a]	1909	1919	1929
3. Leather:			
Iowa	.09700	.18174	1.19361
Minnesota	.09672	.18174	.67641
Wisconsin	.10039	.49079	.16562
Total	.09984	.45334	.19322
4. Rubber:			
Iowa	not determinable	.27913	.44524
Minnesota	not determinable	not determinable	not determinable
Wisconsin	.08556	.40528	.18686
Total	.08556	.36546	.22191
5. Lumber and wood:			
Iowa	.09188	.21455	.20706
Minnesota	.10766	.17711	.19109
Wisconsin	.11187	.26900	.15831
Total	.10851	.23499	.17097
6. Paper and pulp:			
Iowa	.08283	.21211	5.63148
Minnesota	.08651	.17104	.16717
Wisconsin	.09031	.28702	.14865
Total	.17478	.25775	.15356
7. Printing and publishing:			
Iowa	.10229	.25888	.20876
Minnesota	.10257	.23596	.22355
Wisconsin	.10277	.29985	.21453
Total	.10257	.26003	.21379
8. Chemicals:			
Iowa	.07581	.19811	.43179
Minnesota	.09112	.14367	.40059
Wisconsin	.08058	.19684	.41081
Total	.07363	.16697	.41094
9. Stone, clay, and glass:			
Iowa	.08612	.20748	.15092
Minnesota	.08886	.17711	.19227
Wisconsin	.08778	.41019	.28039
Total	.09179	.27452	.17423
10. Metals:			
Iowa	.08795	.19610	.40449
Minnesota	.08653	.17585	.40065
Wisconsin	.08810	.30021	.18771
Total	.08776	.26142	.23781

[a]No separate estimation was made for the "miscellaneous" industries included in the "all industry" total.

Table 2–I.
Ratio of Real Capital Costs in Wisconsin
to Average for Iowa-Minnesota-Wisconsin

Industry group	1909	1919	1929
All industry:	103	117	92
1. Food products	98	110	103
2. Textiles	99	116	67
3. Leather	100	108	86
4. Rubber	100	111	84
5. Lumber and wood	103	114	93
6. Paper and pulp	52	111	97
7. Printing and publishing	100	115	100
8. Chemicals	109	118	100
9. Stone, clay, and glass	96	149	161
10. Metals	100	115	79

SOURCE: Table 2–H.

V

In summary, Wisconsin's set of locational advantages and disadvantages, aside from the clear liability of tax policy, favored the development of the highly productive manufacturing sector characteristic of the other Great Lakes states. But, during the critical years between 1909 and 1929—the period between 1870 and 1950 that found the Great Lakes region growing most rapidly—Wisconsin's growth was decisively inferior to that of the region as a whole.

In the light of Wisconsin's sluggish growth, centered on the relatively poor performance of the metals industries, the generally favorable set of locational conditions for more rapid growth, and the prominent tax constraints placed on Wisconsin's ability to compete for manufacturing capital, taxation emerges as the primary candidate for the critical factor in Wisconsin's relative stagnation during the second and third decades of the century.

Those tax liabilities stemmed from a tax system that applied to manufacturing corporations in a relatively heavy fashion. Even though the level of Wisconsin corporate income taxation seems relatively low by current standards, one should bear in mind that even a small diminution in income can have a rather great impact on the pace of growth if it extends over a long period of time and inhibits processes such as capital formation or entrepreneurial transactions that are absolutely central to the enhancement of social income. That rate of Wisconsin corporate income taxation was, during the years 1911 to 1929, large in relative terms, given the low levels of federal and state corporate income taxation.[15] In the light of the significance of capital costs to the dynamics of economic growth, it is clear that, even if Wisconsin had faced considerable locational disadvantages, tax conditions more favorable to investment would have produced manufacturing expansion more comparable to that of the entire Great Lakes region.

If growth opportunities for the Great Lakes economy had been limited during the first decades of the twentieth century, Wisconsin taxation might have had little long-term effect on the state's position in the national economy. But growth opportunities were extraordinary. The enormous gains possible to that region, including Wisconsin, coupled with Wisconsin tax conditions, meant that Wisconsin specialized more heavily in activities and industries requiring little capital and yielding limited productivity gains while the expansion of heavy industry went forward more rapidly elsewhere in the region. The Wisconsin tax system worked against the forces of the marketplace, which, through refinement of capital markets and the convergence of regional economies, brought into clearer focus the powerful locational advantages of the Great Lakes region.

3

PROGRESSIVES, MANUFACTURERS, AND THE ADOPTION OF INCOME TAXATION

Wisconson's failure to take full advantage of its potential for industrial growth was lodged, perhaps most critically, in the state's policies of taxation. The state government had a large measure of control over the level of industrial taxation, through both income and property levies; with the inception of income taxation, it chose a course that almost certainly inhibited the growth of manufacturing. That change of state policy directed the brunt of the expansion of income taxation and associated increases in property taxation toward the manufacturers. Between 1911 and 1929, the corporate, rather than the individual, income tax generated the vast bulk of income tax revenues; manufacturers carried about two thirds of the corporate tax bill. At the same time, the general exemption of the state's largest corporations—the railroads, most notably —from local property taxation heightened local pressures to tax manufacturers. That exemption, reinforced by changes in the income tax law enacted in 1925, resulted in a significantly higher rate of property taxation to manufacturers in Wisconsin than in other Great Lakes states.

I

The early decades of the twentieth century in industrial America were marked by increased demands for public action to ease social adjustment to urbanization and industrialization. The resultant public action frequently included measures to modify the behavior of manufacturers, especially to increase their contributions to public treasuries. However, the rapidity and the sharpness of the turn toward the increased regulation and taxation of manufacturers was nowhere in the industrial states so pronounced as it was in Wisconsin, as gauged by the character of state tax systems. Until World War I, within the industrial heartland of the nation—the New England, Middle Atlantic, and Great Lakes regions—states either taxed manufacturing corporations with very minimal franchise fees, organization taxes, and state property taxes or left their taxation wholly in the hands of city and town governments. Those towns and cities, usually development-minded, tended, when they were able, to tax manufacturing property at lower rates than property in general. However, during the 1880's and 1890's, as the pressures on cities and towns to provide social-overhead services mounted swiftly, almost all urban governments found it necessary to tax manufacturing property at increasing rates, although the desire to maintain tax conditions favorable to investment continued to be strong.[1] In 1911, Wisconsin broke sharply from even this pattern of stiffer taxation of manufacturing by imposing upon manufacturers a substantial state-level tax; in that year, Wisconsin became the first industrial state to tax significantly income earned from ownership of manufacturing property. The state made its departure even more distinct by, at the same time, leaving the manufacturers subject to local property taxation.

Income taxation by states was by no means new in 1911, but previously such initiatives had been very poorly enforced (as was the Massachusetts tax) and usually had been undertaken by nonindustrial Southern states, which adhered to the hostility toward property taxation developed during the centuries of slavery. No other industrial state moved in Wisconsin's direction until 1915, when Connecticut passed a corporate income tax. Massachusetts and New York followed suit in 1916 and 1917, respectively. Other industrial states,

however, joined this group only at the onset of the Great
Depression, when all states attempted to discover new tax
sources in order to prevent massive deficits.[2] Moreover, Connecticut, Massachusetts, and New York treated corporate
income separately from personal income in that they applied
significantly lower rates to corporations and provided them
with special deductions and exemptions. Further, in New York,
corporations taxed under the income tax acquired substantial
local property tax relief. By 1922, even ignoring the increase
in effective Wisconsin rates produced by more limited deductions and larger surtaxes, Wisconsin's corporate income tax
rate was higher than that in any other state in the nation:
higher even than the 5% achieved by the Non-Partisan
League in North Dakota, higher than in any other major
industrial state (Connecticut's rate was 2%, Massachusetts'
was 2.5% and New York's was 4.5%), and higher than in
any of the other Great Lakes states, which had failed uniformly to pass income tax legislation or to impose property taxation more burdensome to manufacturers. Moreover, by 1922
Wisconsin's rate, although low by post-New Deal federal
standards, was fully 50% of the rate of corporate taxation
imposed by the federal government.[3]

The distinctiveness of Wisconsin's public policy, in both
its scope and its timing, was founded fundamentally upon a
distribution of political power that reflected the relative weakness of manufacturers in the structure of Wisconsin's economy. A similarly weak manufacturing community appeared
also in California, another state highly visible for a reform
episode during the early twentieth century. And both experi-
enced similarly dramatic redirections of regulatory-taxation
interest toward manufacturing.[4] Both California and Wisconsin had smaller manufacturing sectors and contained manufacturing enterprises considerably smaller in scale than did
New York or Massachusetts. All the other Great Lakes states
had developed or were developing (as in the case of Indiana)
manufacturing sectors larger than Wisconsin's, and the scale
of manufacturing was substantially smaller in Wisconsin than

elsewhere in the Great Lakes region.[5] The relatively minor role of manufacturers, particularly large-scale producers, in the economic structure of the state allowed other economic groups to play a relatively greater role in shaping the character of the expanding public sector. Most significant among these competing groups were the agricultural interests, with a set of "class grievances" that urged the redistribution of income from manufacturers to farmers and support for the farmers' competitive position in an industrial marketplace. This pressure produced a blatant effort to use the tax system to redistribute income and to create an agricultural service-state financed in large part by the manufacturers.

The political victory of Wisconsin's agricultural interests, reflected in the adoption of income taxation, arose from the successful effort of a cadre of Republican leaders during the 1890's to reestablish their own leadership in the party and to reaffirm the primacy of their party in Wisconsin. Having been defeated in the early 1890's by Democrats, who capitalized on the rising impact of ethnic and religious associations on political alignments, this Republican leadership devoted itself to developing a kind of secular evangelism that would reestablish the role of economic interests in electoral politics. Although Populism was never a significant force in Wisconsin, rising Republican leaders employed rhetorical and programmatic appeals similar to those advanced by Populists elsewhere; indeed, this redirection of the Republican party in Wisconsin may account for some of the weakness of the Populists there. By the late 1890's, Republican reformers promised economic salvation in an assault upon corporate "tax dodgers," relying on concepts of economic morality that had traditionally appealed to farmers since the victory of the Jacksonian general property tax. Beyond the attack on corporations, this redefinition of the Republican party program included the adoption of a positive state policy designed to solve the problems of specialized agriculture within an industrial economy. Although such a program had considerable appeal in Wisconsin even in buoyant times, the relatively depressed years of the 1890's, provoking fiscal crises and trapping farmers between high fixed costs and low prices, provided particularly favorable economic conditions for recasting the Republican party program along class lines. Consequently, Wisconsin voting began to shift from an earlier pattern that, during the early 1890's, had highlighted ethnic and religious differences, to a pattern that responded more closely to differences of income level and occupation. In 1900, this new Republican leadership turned the political corner to success with the nomination and election of Governor Robert M. La Follette.[6]

Redirecting Wisconsin politics toward a set of agricultural interests coincided with the growing nationwide search for an alternative to general property taxation. The social need for an alternative became more acutely and widely felt as industrialization and urbanization proceeded and the difficulties involved in identifying property became more intense, with property growing more "personal" and "intangible" in character. Early nineteenth-century assessment procedures were simply inadequate to expose and determine the value of money, credits, notes, bonds, stocks, and mortgages. The shrinking tax base of the depression years of the 1890's only intensified the quest for improvement in the application of old taxes or for development of new taxes. Concern for tax equality appeared in every industrial state, producing an array of suggested solutions, including improved property-assessment procedures, exemption of certain classes of property difficult to assess, the classification of property into categories taxed at different rates, the separation of state and local revenue systems to eliminate competitive underassessment by counties seeking to reduce their shares of state property taxes, and the enactment of substitute taxes, such as inheritance taxes, special corporation taxes, and the income tax.[7]

In Wisconsin, dissatisfaction with personal property taxation also became widespread during the late nineteenth century and grew particularly intense during the 1890's, but it had a distinctly more rural focus than in other industrial states.[8] A set of municipal reformers, seeking a more even distribution of urban taxes and a more buoyant tax base, contributed significantly to the critique of the general property tax posed in the 1890's, but the political force behind that critique was heavily rural.[9] Thus, a central conclusion of even the urban-based temporary Tax Commission of 1897–1898 was that "There is perhaps no class of people who feel the direct burden of taxation more keenly than the farmers"; and, in that context, the Commission heavily criticized the adequacy of the assessment of intangibles in the state.[10] In building support among farmers for the emerging Republican reform coalition, Robert M. La Follette, in 1897, anticipated the findings of the Commission with a critique that asserted that the valuation of horses exceeded that of intangibles by more than $5 million. The obvious solution was to find a means of shifting the burden of taxation from farm property to intangibles.[11]

The means chosen to shift the tax burden in Wisconsin also revealed the rural focus of the movement to reform general property taxation. Only five years after the 1898 Tax Commission report, Wisconsin embarked upon the process of constitutional amendment required to adopt state income taxation. Only in agricultural areas of industrial states was support strong for the income tax as an alternative to personal property taxation. Throughout the more industrial areas of the nation the belief prevailed that the income tax, whether adopted at the federal or state level, would redistribute income toward farmers, as farmers owned relatively large amounts of tangible property and earned incomes that were either low or very difficult to measure. Accordingly, relatively more agricultural Wisconsin had been traditionally a source of significant support for federal income taxation; it contributed to the adoption of the Civil War income tax, from 1862 to 1872, and the short-lived levy imposed in 1894.[12] The state did not move to income taxation immediately after La Follette's election only because of lingering urban opposition, particularly among the tax experts, who would have to assume responsibility for drafting and implementing such a tax, and, most importantly, the short-term preoccupation of the new Republican coalition of the 1890's with other tax reform endeavors.

Throughout the nation, tax experts, with a disposition favorable to urban, middle-class concerns, usually looked dimly on state income taxation as a tool for reform of the general property tax system. Simply, they thought that income taxation would prove unusually favorable to farm interests or considered the tax inadequate by the canons of political and economic efficiency.[13] The strongest, most persuasive arguments in opposition to state income taxation during the first decade of the century were those of Edwin R. A. Seligman of Columbia University. He suspected that concealing income from state assessors was easier than camouflaging personal property, that the national or regional nature of industry made the segregation of corporate earnings by states a virtual impossibility, and that an effective state income tax would result in a disadvantage for the state in attracting corporate investment.[14] Consequently, Seligman believed in the clear superiority of national income taxation.[15] In Wisconsin, the experts who were skeptical of the applicability of income taxation to the problems of state taxation included Richard T. Ely. Delos O. Kinsman, a graduate student of Ely's at the University of Wisconsin, and Kossuth K. Kennan, a Milwaukee proponent of steeper utility taxation. Ely had earlier advocated the adoption of a state income tax in his 1886 investigation of state and local taxes for the Maryland Tax Commission. But, by the late 1890's, Ely had concluded that the income tax was "better adapted for national purposes than for state," and in the 1901 edition of his economics textbook he dropped any mention of state income taxation.[16] Reinforcing Ely's revised position were the Kinsman and Kennan histories of income taxation, which concluded that the states had been largely unsuccessful in their scattered efforts at income taxation.[17] As a result, in 1898 and even as late as in 1909, Wisconsin tax commissions tended to be cool toward the income tax as an effective means for achieving greater equity in the state's tax system.[18] Nonetheless, the opposition of tax experts toward income taxation was not a crucial obstruction in Wisconsin. Once the Republican reformers had exhausted other, more obvious vehicles for restructuring or supplementing the property tax, they moved expeditiously toward the income taxation and innovation in the taxation of manufacturers. In the process, they found tax experts willing to cooperate in promoting their experiment.

Before the Republicans brought to power in 1900 could consider income taxation, they had to turn first toward two more visible modes of tax reform, both of which, in principle, closely resembled the old general property tax.[19] In the first place, the anticorporate enthusiasms of the 1890's focused attention on increasing the tax contributions of those corporations with the longest history of antagonism from agricultural interests, the railroads, and led to efforts to develop property taxes that would reach these particular corporations. Not only were railroads subject to farmer attacks as providers of transportation services but they were obvious targets for urban tax reformers as well, given their visibility as Wisconsin's largest corporate bodies. Indeed, urban reformers participating in the new Republican coalition saw the enhanced taxation of railroads and, more generally, all utilities as central to solution of the fiscal problems of the cities during the 1890's.[20] Even the manufacturers favored tax reform in the 1890's because heavier taxation of other corporations meant a reduction of the tax burden on manufacturers imposed by property taxes.[21] The most visible outcome of this initial corporate tax reform thrust was the adoption, in 1903, of *ad valorem* property taxation of railroads.

The second source of delay in adopting income taxation was the logical interest in strengthening the existing system of personal property taxation before adopting an untried form of taxation. The source of that effort was interest, fed by the agricultural depression of the 1890's, to tax all lenders of agricultural capital more fully than was possible under the existing personal property tax. While the primary lenders, the banking corporations, were already well taxed under the general property tax, the property tax system reached only incompletely the assets of noninstitutional lenders, such as prosperous farmers or real estate agents.[22] Thus, a primary tax reform effort of La Follette's first administration was to centralize property tax assessment procedures under a permanent Tax Commission devoted to pressuring local assessors to improve the assessment of intangibles. As a result of the assessment drive, between 1901 and 1902, the assessed value of personal property increased more than 40% and the value of "money and credits" more than doubled.[23]

The serious movement toward income taxation began when the more conservative reform of personal property taxation foundered on political shoals. The success of the assessment drive led noninstitutional lenders to seek property tax relief for themselves, during the 1903 legislative session, through the exemption of all intangibles, but particularly mortgages, from the general property tax. Because many of the individuals reached by the improved property taxation, both farmers and urban real estate interests, had supported the reordering of the Republican party and contributed to the new coalition, the desire of noninstitutional lenders for credit exemption rent the La Follette forces.[24] Opposed were not only the small-farmer component at the heart of La Follette's support but also the banking community, which vigorously opposed credit exemption as providing an unfair advantage to noninstitutional lenders. The contending interests were sufficiently heated in their disagreement to obstruct enactment of the *ad valorem* taxation of railroads then before the legislature. Representing small farmers and bankers was one of the central figures in the new Republican alignment, Tax Commissioner Nils P. Haugen, long-time political leader of the agricultural Norwegian population and himself a substantial bank investor in his home region of Pierce County.[25] Haugen, perhaps acting on behalf of La Follette, took it upon himself to resolve the conflicting interests of small lenders, on the one

hand, and bankers and small farmers, on the other hand. He
did so by both supporting the proposal to exempt credits from
property taxation and strongly endorsing a state income tax.[26]

Although Haugen was the first state politician of influence
to make such an income tax endorsement, residual support
among farmers from the federal income tax campaigns was
strong enough for the legislature to initiate immediately the
process of constitutional amendment to permit state income
taxation. The prospect of income taxation was sufficiently ap-
pealing to small farmers to allow the legislature to exempt
mortgages from general property taxation. Not only did Haugen's compromise restore the coalition of reform forces, it
allowed that coalition to enact the *ad valorem* taxation of railroads by breaking the legislature log-jam over credit taxation.
Thus, in 1903, the legislature concluded the first major thrust
of the Republican tax reforms and, at the same time, began a
new drive that would result in a more rigorous taxation of
manufacturers.

With the endorsement of the legislature and the Republican statewide leadership, including Governor La Follette as
well as Nils Haugen, the income tax movement encountered
no substantive obstacles. The delay of final passage of the constitutional amendment until 1908 reflected only the cumber-
some process of amendment. The two-to-one victory of income
taxation in the mandatory popular referendum of 1908 revealed
a continued popular support, particularly in poorer agricultural
districts, for income taxation.[27]

Despite the decisive endorsement of the principle of income taxation, the public and even experts in tax affairs had
only a poorly developed concept of what specific provisions such
taxation should include. The most prominent self-appointed
income tax expert, Nils Haugen, who had a penchant for the
invocation of academic authority, involved himself in income
tax literature apparently far more to enhance his intellectual
credentials among politicians than to enlighten public dis-
course.[28] Among the Wisconsin academic community, only
one tax expert, Thomas Sewell Adams of the University, de-

veloped an interest in income taxation during these transitional years, 1903–1908. Even he saw the tax simply as a replacement for the entire personal property tax; he lent no consideration to the specific manner in which the tax might apply to business activity.[29] By 1907, Haugen had endorsed the substitution of income for personal property taxation suggested by Adams but made no mention of the fact that the income tax, by replacing the personal property tax, would shift a larger part of the tax base to those urban taxpayers, especially manufacturers, who were taxed only under the general property tax.[30] If, in 1908, Haugen and other experts and politicians saw the tax as anything more complicated than a more effective means of taxing "capitalists," there is no evidence to that effect. And, if the manufacturers saw an imminent attempt to tax their profits, they did not make their sentiments public. The scattered early critics of the income tax considered it to be a variety of personal, rather than business, taxation.[31]

Eventually, between 1909 and 1911, progressive politicians focused their attention on the manufacturing corporations as they broadened and deepened their concept of income taxation and, at the same time, sought to define public issues even more sharply in class terms. In response, the manufacturers began to seek to shape their political environment, but their heightened awareness did little to reduce the momentum already developed by 1909, despite the vague public definition of the content of income taxation. Once public attention had become riveted on the communal role of large manufacturing corporations, Wisconsin progressives, supported by the political ineptitude of the manufacturers and the indifference of politically powerful nonmanufacturing corporations to the plight of the manufacturers, rapidly altered the state's tax system to redistribute income away from manufacturing.

II

By the conclusion of the 1909 legislative session, the Wisconsin income tax movement focused squarely on increasing the contribution of the state's manufacturers to the public revenues. In part, this focus was the result of the internal logic of the effort to tax incomes rather than "intangible" personal property that fell under the general property tax; the "intangible" property of manufacturing corporations, as well as that held by individual capitalists, lay largely beyond the reach of the property tax assessor. Once the movement to tax credits pointed toward presumed social sins of manufacturers, progressives had an opportunity to mobilize traditional Wisconsin anti-corporate passions. The spectacular growth of manufacturing corporations had become very marked in the expansive first decade of the century and created an opportunity for Wisconsin progressives to capitalize on the class basis of their movement, just when they had exhausted the issue of railroad taxation and regulation. Further, the federal government's move to tax incomes intensified, to a significant extent as a result of the energies of Senator La Follette. The national debate reinforced the discussion in Wisconsin, and La Follette's arguments both advanced the cause of state income taxation and centered interest on income taxation of the manufacturers.

In 1909, when Congress approved the Sixteenth Amendment on behalf of income taxation, it also enacted a tax on corporate incomes. La Follette had vigorously supported federal income taxation, arguing that its fundamental appeal was its ability to redistribute wealth, especially the wealth corporations had "expropriated" from the public at large. Phasing out the tariff would reduce the tax burden on the consumer, La Follette suggested, while enacting an income tax would shift that burden to large corporations. He described the income tax movement as "a struggle to lay the foundation upon which we shall finally create a MORE EQUITABLE SYSTEM OF TAXATION. Much of the vast wealth which privilege has taken from the toil of the many, for the benefit of the few, can be forced to render to the government that which it owes to the government in no other way." When La Follette's followers in Wisconsin came to consider state income taxation, they used almost the identical arguments. For example, John

J. Blaine, Assemblyman from Boscobel and future progressive Governor, maintained that corporations would not be able to pass on a state income tax to consumers and hence the tax would "greatly relieve the over-burdened consumer and place the tax where it belongs."[32]

The first state income tax proposal, appearing in February, 1909, under the names of C. A. Ingram, a Republican Assemblyman from Pepin county in La Follette country along the Mississippi, and Paul Husting, a Democratic senator from agricultural Dodge county, was so poorly drafted that the legislators quickly buried it in committee for the duration of the session. But that first bill's provisions for a centrally administered tax, a graduated rate structure for both personal and corporate incomes, and the lack of a distinction between personal and business taxation aroused substantive opposition from the state's manufacturers.[33] In February of 1910, in anticipation of further legislative initiatives, William George Bruce, former Milwaukee Tax Commissioner and Secretary of the Milwaukee Merchants and Manufacturers Association (MMMA), lauded the manufacturers' offensive by asserting that Wisconsin should not adopt an income tax before a considerable number of states were ready to join. Advancing an argument the manufacturers would rigidly adhere to for over 20 years, Bruce declared that, given Wisconsin's isolation in adopting a rigorous income tax, the result of such a bill passing would be a flight of "capital and industries out of the state and into adjoining states." Bruce declined to suggest any reasonable grounds for compromise between proponents of income taxation and those who represented manufacturers.[34]

At the same time, the MMMA drew up its own report on income taxation. Under the authorship of Bruce and Kossuth K. Kennan, a tax lawyer who had crusaded for a Tax Commission and had written a critical history of income taxation, the report provided an elaborate rendition of Bruce's views.[35] The MMMA advised the legislature that "taxation is a factor in interstate commerce in as much as it enters into the cost of production" and "since the manufacturers of one state must compete with those of another," it would be "unwise for any one state to place a heavier burden upon its producers than is placed by adjoining states." The state could not prevent "industrial enterprises as well as individuals enjoying large incomes . . . from removing to states where the tax laws were more acceptable." The manufacturers advised that "the progressive community should invite the investment of capital rather than drive it away."[36]

The organized opposition of the Association to income taxation reflected a reorganization in 1910 that gave the larger Milwaukee manufacturers control of the Association, with the most prominent role played by the machinery manufacturers. General Otto H. Falk, vice-president of the Falk Corporation and later president of Allis-Chalmers, was in command of the MMMA, while Paul D. Carpenter, a lawyer for the Falk Corporation, was chairman of its Committee on Legislation. The most prominent members of the legislative committee represented the International Harvester Company, The Filer and Stowell Co., Allis-Chalmers, and the Milwaukee Metal Trades and Founders Association. Those manufacturers, although among the largest in the state and reaching interstate markets, participated in highly competitive industries.[37] Consequently, they had become acutely concerned with the threat increased taxes posed to their competitive abilities and to their massive and rapidly growing capital commitments to Wisconsin. Although, in the course of the following decades, businessmen throughout the nation would resort routinely and indiscriminately to arguments threatening retardation of economic growth whenever state governments threatened to raise their taxes, these Wisconsin manufacturers realistically forecast the state's future competitive position under the income tax system. Although no significant number of "foot-loose" industries moved to sunnier political climes, the Wisconsin income tax, coupled with associated increase in the property tax, would heighten the relative cost of capital to manufacturers and thus retard investment in manufacturing and restrict economic growth through inhibiting investment in industries, such as that of metal products fabrication, that were central to the continued strong growth of the state.

The Milwaukee group of manufacturers proceeded to create a state-wide body to bring continuity and widened support for their political efforts in opposing what they expected to be a sustained drive toward income taxation. In 1910, the Milwaukee manufacturers under Falk revived the Wisconsin Manufacturers Association (WMA) by recruiting representatives from the Nekoosa-Edwards Paper Company, the La Crosse Rubber Works, the Simmons Manufacturing Company of Kenosha, the J. I. Case Threshing Machine Co. of Racine, the Wisconsin Brewers Association, the Bolens Co. of Port Washington, the Fairbanks-Morse Co. of Beloit, the Phoenix Manufacturing Co. (a textile firm) from Eau Claire, the Gisholt Co. (a machine-tool producer) of Madison, and Kimberly-Clark Co. of Neenah. The broader group of manufacturers, representing the largest manufacturers domiciled in the state, all produced for highly competitive interstate markets and therefore emphasized their fundamental objective to seek "constructive" legislation to "encourage industrial effort." The state, they asserted, should simply seek to render for the industrial development of the state "the same service which has been rendered for the agricultural." This wider group of manufacturers, in the succeeding twenty years, would lead the opposition to income taxation and continue to reiterate the arguments of the Milwaukee group. With certain minor elaborations, the manufacturers of the WMA would continue to stress the danger of "progressive" tax legislation in shackling investment and would persist in an unbending posture of hostility to compromise.[38]

The WMA represented those manufacturers most concerned about the future of Wisconsin taxation—those manufacturers with very large capital stakes in Wisconsin but with very little manufacturing activity outside the state's boundaries. Almost all of those corporations were domiciled in Wisconsin and conducted their production in a single community. Most engaged in the manufacture of metal products, including machine tools and fabricated metal products, electrical equipment, agricultural machinery, paper and paper products, and beer. The manufacturers not represented fell largely into two categories: (1) the nation's greatest producers who had licenses to do business in Wisconsin and perhaps even owned branch plants there, as did General Motors, for example, and (2) the very small-scale manufacturers such as those who processed dairy products. While the former expected to experience a diminished return on their Wisconsin investments, they, in contrast with the "Wisconsin manufacturers," would find it far easier to shift investment plans to favor other Great Lakes locations; during the first decades of the century, and especially the 1920's, the large, multidivisional, interstate corporations were becoming increasingly sensitive to interstate differentials in tax costs as a part of a larger program of rationalized cost control.[39] Partly as a consequence of that marketplace flexibility, these manufacturers chose to avoid meddling in state politics. The group of small-scale dairymen and cheese producers also failed to register significant opposition to the Wisconsin income tax, anticipating benefits from the rates at the low end of the scale of graduated income tax rates.

Despite the broad umbrella of the WMA, the large Milwaukee manufacturers provided the initial leadership, both intellectual and political, in opposition to the threatened income tax. The influential Milwaukee group contained a majority of Wisconsin's largest manufacturers, who were more accustomed to organizing for political influence and more aware of the danger of state government siphoning off revenues from urban governments and increasing the relative tax burden on manufacturers. The state income tax threatened to augment their tax load without relieving them, as had earlier special taxes on other corporations, from potentially more burdensome local and county taxation. The foremost spokesman for the manufacturers on this particular issue had long been William George Bruce who, as Milwaukee Tax Commissioner during the 1890's, became concerned with the increasing taxes borne by Milwaukee manufacturers and concluded that the source of the problem was the exemption of the property of nonmanufacturing corporations from local taxation. Bruce had explained that "The gross injustice under which the city now suffers is that it does not receive its proportion of the taxes which it creates." More specifically, Milwaukee had "within its limits vast property holdings which yield a large tax return, none of which finds its way into Milwaukee's treasury," because "the large corporations, with few exceptions," paid their taxes directly into the state treasury, while Milwaukee, "which affords these vast properties all the protection of a municipality, receives nothing." One result had been the imposition of a heavier burden on the manufacturer and the likelihood of inhibiting Milwaukee's development since "the manufacturer who competes with the manufacturer in other cities must have the same favorable tax rate."[40]

As Bruce suggested, the Wisconsin nonmanufacturing corporations had succeeded in keeping their tax burden under control. The utility corporations (including railroads), especially, had become accustomed to favorable results in influencing tax politics. For example, the state had taxed steam railroads on their gross receipts beginning in 1854; the public's share went to the state treasury, and the railroads were exempt from local property taxation. The railroads found that exemption particularly desirable during the depressed years of the 1890's when local governments vigorously sought new sources of revenue in dealing with fiscal crises. In 1903, progressive reformers applied *ad valorem* taxation, or taxation using property value rather than income or receipts as a base, to steam railroads but failed to restore any local control over railroad taxation and thus failed to provide an ideal opportunity for localities to modify the property tax burden of manufacturers. Indeed, the railroads appear to have welcomed the adoption of the new basis of taxation, with their buoyant incomes following the economic recovery beginning at the end of the 1890's, the ominous increase of the license fee enacted in 1897, and the sharp increase in that fee threatened by the most fervently antirailroad progressives in 1901.[41] The street railways enjoyed a similarly favored position after 1895, when the state applied the method of taxing steam railroads, including the exemption from local property taxation, to urban transit systems and their connected utilities.[42] The extension of *ad valorem* taxation to street railways also preserved the favoritism extended to large utility combines, as the light, heat, and power companies not owned in connection with a street railway had to carry the local tax rate. Thus, the Milwaukee Electric Railway and Light Company, which owned an electric lighting system, was taxed at the average state rate while the competing gas light company was taxed at a local rate, which was invariably higher. The tendency to exempt large utilities from local taxation and to tax them at a lower state-wide rate resulted in greater pressure on the manufacturers to increase their share of local property taxes. It is clear that, while the thrust of the tax movement in Wisconsin had been anticorporate in the 1890's, progressives ultimately accommodated to the power, both economic and political, of the utilities. The adoption of *ad valorem* taxation was a distinct compromise that was quite amenable to the interests of the corporations taxed.[43]

The political strength of the utilities, in contrast to that of the manufacturers, emerged subsequently in the transformation of the income tax concept between the abortive 1909 income tax proposal and the introduction of the first bill of the 1911 session. The 1909 proposal had elicited opposition not only from the manufacturers but from the other classes of corporations as well, as the proposed act would have taxed the income of all corporations. But having conducted hearings around the state, having mobilized support of tax experts, and having tested the temperature of political waters, supporters of the income tax left only the manufacturers and merchants within the ambit of the corporation income tax. The income tax draft presented in January of 1911 provided an exemption for banks and trust companies and, most significantly, for companies paying license fees and *ad valorem* taxes, including steam railroads and insurance companies.[44] Yet, corporations paying income taxes were granted no exemptions for local taxation of real property.

Manufacturers, with their relatively concentrated property holdings, preferred to have taxation controlled locally, while the utilities, particularly the steam railroads, with their more widely dispersed property, preferred state taxation and regulation. While the railroads had welcomed a more uniform tax system, the manufacturers resisted state-wide control over corporate taxation and found that the income tax threatened them with both state and local tax increases. The utilities, by opposing their inclusion under the system of income taxation yet not opposing such taxation of the manufacturers, effectively lent their support to the new anticorporate initiative of the progressives. The benefits the utilities would garner from the state and local taxation of manufacturing were obvious, and the utilities had a generation of experience with special regulatory and tax policies upon which to draw for successful strategies and tactics appropriate to dealing with reformers. The result, in part, was that the primary thrust of the income tax legislation as proposed in the first 1911 bill was to increase the governmental contribution of the manufacturers without extending any compensations; progressives had proved more responsive to the interests of the other corporations.

In 1911, manufacturers responded to the revised tax proposals by complaining that the income tax, if it failed to provide sufficient property tax relief, would inhibit interstate competition. One representative from Sheboygan argued in February hearings that because the tangible property of manufacturers, their plants and equipment, was exposed to the assessor, manufacturers ran the risk of being taxed on more than their net worth.[45] The Milwaukee manufacturers explicitly shared this fear of increased property taxation and objected to the levying of new taxes on top of property taxes already swollen, they were certain, by the state's limitations on local property taxation of corporations and the state's skimming of corporate tax revenues.[46]

The manufacturers also added a new criticism of the tax,

one that predicted severe enforcement problems. Paul D. Carpenter and Harry Bolens, vice-president of the WMA, emphasized the ability of corporations, especially corporations owned outside the state, to evade the tax. Carpenter pointed out that Illinois owners, for instance, could form a sales corporation outside of Wisconsin to purchase the product of the Wisconsin company and drain off Wisconsin profits. (In fact, this method did become a popular, probably the most popular means, of attempting to avoid Wisconsin income taxes.[47]) He made his point both to ridicule income taxation as profitless to the state and, more importantly, to frighten progressives with necessity of producing a vast and costly new bureaucracy.[48] However, Carpenter's preaching only led income tax supporters to return their bill to Charles McCarthy's Legislative Reference Library for redrafting, directing him to pay more careful attention to the creation of an adequate administrative structure, precisely with the objective of insuring that the tax reached all manufacturing profits. An indication of the success that McCarthy, the other experts (especially Delos O. Kinsman, who assisted McCarthy), and the legislators enjoyed was the ability of their Tax Commission to close the loophole that Carpenter had exposed so candidly in 1911.

In their 1911 assault on the proposed tax, the prominent manufacturers never allowed their political antagonists an opportunity for meaningful compromise. The only manufacturer suggestion with any possibility for promoting compromise was the pledge of support for Wisconsin's ratification of the federal income tax amendment. The manufacturers consistently asserted that such a tax was preferable to a state tax.[49] But that action hardly constituted a major concession; although the manufacturers did follow through on their promise, they had little to do with the state's overwhelming ratification and, subsequently, played no part in the framing of a federal tax.[50] Of even less significance was the support by the manufacturers, in the final stages of legislative deliberation, of a move to submit the tax to the public for approval in a referendum. The interest of the manufacturers was transparently to provide themselves with a fighting chance to defeat the measure; although they had some significant allies, particularly the Socialists, who were unsure of the effects of placing another tax burden on industry, the proposal failed to pass the legislature.[51] In effect, the manufacturers proved unable, in 1911, to develop strategies appropriate to their relatively weak political position. As a consequence, they weakened their political situation even further. Behind their political ineptitude lay not only the strength of the antimanufacturer combination but also a lack of political experience and an exceptionally narrow social vision.

Although compromise was a more realistic objective for the manufacturers than total victory, they were, in part, simply following the suit of the progressives, who never opened areas for cooperation with the manufacturers. The tax experts, who might have been expected to take seriously the consensus of tax economists that a state income tax, if not accompanied by tax relief, was likely to retard a state's economic progress, either reinforced the progressive desire to tax the manufacturers more heavily or, if they did suggest compromise proposals, acted in response to a calculation of the political, rather than the economic setting of the tax. In the latter category, Professor Thomas S. Adams, in 1911, suggested the levying of only a low flat-rate to corporations, a lower rate of taxation on out-of-state income, and the exemption of interest payments from corporate income taxation. He made those proposals not to avoid placing Wisconsin manufacturers at a competitive disadvantage but to mollify businessmen and thus speed up the adoption of income taxation.[52] Indeed, Adams intended to ignore the competitive position of businessmen under the proposed 1911 legislation. He may have done so because he believed that other states would follow Wisconsin's good example and adopt corporate income taxes. Certainly he did suggest the possibility of more widespread adoption of state income taxation. But he made that suggestion only in the context of attempting to develop support among hostile economists for the Wisconsin tax program and, in addition, Adams dismissed the problem of "migration of capital" even under the circumstance of uneven state income taxation.[53] More generally, there is no evidence that, in 1911, proponents of Wisconsin's income tax, including Charles McCarthy, cared particularly about the future influence of their income tax innovation. In that year, McCarthy's primary consideration was the configuration of political power around an economic issue he evaluated simply in terms of communal equity.[54] With his incomparable sensitivity to Wisconsin political reality, he uniformly rejected Adams' political advice as an opinion that exaggerated the strength of the manufacturer opposition to the income tax.

Despite the reservations of Adams, the very rigorous McCarthy bill, which had been prompted by the protests of the manufacturers, emerged as the basic income tax blueprint. Most significantly, the McCarthy bill rested the income tax even more squarely on the corporations than had earlier versions. It created assessment districts larger than individual counties, provided for the administration of those districts by state-appointed, state-paid assessors, empowered the Tax Commission to double the rate of taxation in the case of fraudulent corporate behavior (a higher rate of penalty than for fraud perpetrated by individuals), taxed corporate interest payments, and, most originally, permitted taxpayers to offset their personal property taxes against income taxes.[55] The last provision promised to reduce or eliminate the impact of the income tax on agricultural districts. The old general property tax reached the tangible personal property of farmers—farm animals and equipment, most notably—far more completely than the corresponding property of manufacturers, such as inventories.[56] McCarthy and Kinsman calculated that most farmers with personal property would be able to cancel out their income tax obligation. Thus, the income tax would be an additional burden primarily on nonfarm taxpayers, whose personal property was taxed less heavily. To promote the virtues of the McCarthy-Kinsman bill, Senator Edward Kileen of the special Income Tax Committee predicted that with the personal property offset, the state would receive but little tax revenue from farming areas and, thus, that the income tax would be an additional burden primarily on urban taxpayers.[57] More generally, proponents of the new bill argued that the central intent of the measure was to "equalize" revenues, rather than to raise new revenues. They fully expected the income tax to take the place of the personal property tax if it proved to be successful in raising revenue; the object of the tax reform in 1911 was simply to shift a greater share of the costs of government to certain urban taxpayers, especially the manufacturers.

The enactment of the McCarthy bill in June, 1911, after only minor modifications, reflected the failure of legislators representing the more agricultural portions of the state to explore significant areas for compromise between the progressives and the manufacturers. Although one can not be certain what political results the manufacturers would have obtained by accepting the principle of state income taxation, in 1911 no significant support materialized among legislators on behalf of modifications in the basic law that would have been favorable to the manufacturers. Only a few Republicans were opposed to the tax, and they were the representatives of the Lake Michigan and Rock River industrial cities, particularly Kenosha and Janesville, that were close to the Illinois-Wisconsin line and would face more direct competition with neighboring cities such as Waukegan and Rockford.[58] The Democrats, having a more urban base of power in the industrial Fox River Valley and Milwaukee and hedging against an unfavorable public reaction to income taxation in the future, proposed levying a flat 1% tax and maintaining the existing administrative apparatus for assessments. However, the Assembly buried that proposal by more than a two-to-one vote.[59] The Socialists also tended to oppose the tax as enacted, supporting the unsuccessful effort to send the McCarthy bill to a referendum, but the Socialist minority was too small to place the coalition of dissident Republicans, conservative Democrats, and Socialists in the majority.[60] Finally, no support for the position of the manufacturers, as represented by the MMMA and the WMA, materialized among other business groups. Other corporations undoubtedly hoped to see part of their state tax burden passed to the manufacturers if they escaped from the corporate tax. In fact, a more centralized tax system promised to enhance the assessment of local and state property values and thus, to the benefit of the utilities and railroads, increase even further the contribution of manufacturers to state and local tax revenues. As for the bankers, who were to be covered by the new income tax, many had good reason to prefer income taxation to property tax.[61] Thus, significant economic differences split the business community of Wisconsin over tax issues, and the manufacturers found themselves isolated as the weakest corporate group in the Wisconsin polity.

The political weakness of the manufacturers appeared clearly in the last round of fighting before adoption of the tax; the manufacturers bulldozed ahead in direct opposition but found the legislature coolly ignoring them. Thus, in a May public hearing on the final bill, the manufacturers discovered "only empty benches to talk to." Apparently by progressive design, the hearing conflicted with both a Democratic banquet in Madison and a Republican caucus called by Governor Francis E. McGovern for the same evening.[62] Then, as the final bill emerged from committee after technical revisions, Otto Falk, Chairman of the Executive Committee of the WMA, organized a massive lobbying effort, bringing large delegations from Milwaukee and outlying industrial centers to Madison and pressuring the Governor directly.[63] Despite that enterprise, the final enactment maintained a graduated rate structure with a 6% maximum, preserved the highly centralized administrative apparatus, created the personal property tax offset, and exempted the utilities (including the railroads), and any other corporation taxed by the state under special legislation, from income taxation.[64] The final discussion in June surrounding the act, particularly in the Senate, focused not on the taxation of manufacturers but upon the impact of the tax on agriculture. The proponents of the tax, usually explicit representatives of farming interests, were candid in predicting, with considerable accuracy, that "under this bill, the farmers would not have to pay an income tax."[65]

4

THE MANUFACTURERS AND THE
TESTING OF THE INCOME TAX, 1911-1929

I

When Governor Francis E. McGovern signed the income tax into law in July, 1911, the Wisconsin manufacturers initiated various approaches to blunt the impact of the new measure on the conduct of their business, but they also initiated a record of political failure that prevailed until the 1920's. Initially, the most obviously promising strategy was to maneuver the administration of the tax into conformity with their interests. The previous success of the railroads in gaining decisive leverage over the machinery for the regulation and taxation of railroads may have encouraged the threatened, but politically naive, manufacturers.[1] The manufacturers, however, failed to win any victories in the contests with the tax bureaucracy.

From their first reporting of income in 1912, the manufacturers consistently sought to explore every ambiguity of the tax law, both in communication with the Tax Commission and the Assessors of Income and by legal action; and, judged by instances of penalty rate invocation, some manufacturers went further to violate the law knowingly.[2] But despite their persistent efforts, the manufacturers were unable to enlist sympathetic supporters on the Tax Commission. That body of gubernatorial appointees, possessing total responsibility for

administering the corporate tax, proved to be inflexibly opposed
to the requests of the manufacturers. The Commissioners usually had strong political ties with income tax champions, were
generally lawyers by occupation, were always committed to
making the tax an administrative success, accepted consistently
the intellectual defense of the tax advanced by its political
friends, quarreled only rarely with the prevailing political
judgment that Wisconsin's polity could safely ignore the
manufacturers' interests, and tended to have political origins
outside the state's industrial centers.[3]

When the manufacturers presented the Tax Commission
with a request for a favorable interpretation of a dubious point
of law, the Tax Commission invariably ruled in favor of the
state, with the objective of maximizing revenues. By May,
1912, for example, the Commission had ruled that almost all
machinery would be assessed as real property rather than as
personal property, in contrast with the practice in other industrial states. By so ruling, the Commission prevented manufacturers from offsetting property taxes on machinery against
income taxes, despite the complaints of Otto Falk, William
George Bruce, and others that the result was "double taxation."[4] Also, the Tax Commission immediately sought to
close the potential loophole of a Wisconsin-incorporated company setting up an out-of-state sales corporation to drain off
Wisconsin profits otherwise subject to the income tax. Although one company, U.S. Glue, took the Tax Commissioners
to the United States Supreme Court in its attempt to do this,
the Commissioners meanwhile continued to tax profits made
on all sales of goods manufactured in Wisconsin by Wisconsin
companies; in 1918, the highest court confirmed the progressive
judgment that such taxation did not interfere unconstitutionally
with interstate commerce.

More generally, the Tax Commission always scrutinized
intensely the returns of corporations, particularly the largest
corporations, in the home office, frequently making an effort
to obtain supportive information and data. Then, beginning
in 1919, the Tax Commission began an even more forceful

effort to go behind the reported record of the corporations by fully auditing their books. Supporting the Commission, the legislature spent generously to create a field auditing staff and, in general, to facilitate field auditing. In that auditing, the Commission did not hesitate to examine thoroughly the books of any corporation, including even the large interstate-corporations, regardless of where they were incorporated or where their home offices were located. To support those audits, the Commission occasionally doubled the rate of taxation on concealed income, which was its prerogative, and always charged a substantial rate of interest on additional taxes assessed, as much as 10% for most of the 1920's.

The Commission reinforced its assessment and reassessment decisions through its function as a board of review. Despite manufacturer protests, the state created no separate, independent review body during the period; consequently, the Tax Commission served both an executive and a judicial function, not only enforcing the income tax law but also reviewing its own enforcement. Claiming, in effect, that the Tax Commission would turn from a partisan, aggressive search for more revenue to an impartial interpretation of the law, the Commission advised one field auditor that "as the corporation has the right of hearing an appeal, you are naturally expected to resolve questions of doubt in favor of the state." An aggrieved corporation, of course, had further access to the courts, but only a rare firm pursued this course, not only because of the costs involved but also because Wisconsin courts generally adopted a favorable attitude toward the decisions of the Tax Commission in its review capacity. Thus, the manufacturers found themselves impotent in conditioning the administration of the income tax law; they were unable to duplicate the success of the utilities in turning the instruments of taxation to their own advantage.[5]

II

Consistently rebuffed in assaulting the progressive administrative structure, the manufacturers dwelt instead on electoral and legislative politics to reduce the competitive disadvantage created by Wisconsin taxation. After 1911, they often took their case to the public, much as they had advocated in proposing a referendum, and continued to work in the legislature for the modification of the original enactment and the prevention of further initiatives. But not until 1925, after their most unequivocal defeat, did manufacturers begin to explore seriously the possibilities for approaching Wisconsin politicians with a disposition amenable to compromise and the formation of alliances with dissident sectors of the progressive community. Partly as a consequence, the issue of the taxation of manufacturers remained at the center of Wisconsin politics for almost two decades, in contrast to the receding issues of the regulation and taxation of nonmanufacturing corporations.

As early as the state elections of 1912, the manufacturers turned to the public, reasonably confident of receiving the support which they were absolutely certain they deserved. Working through the Milwaukee Democratic organization, the larger manufacturers, the leaders of the WMA and the MMMA, captured the gubernatorial nomination for a popular former football hero of the University of Wisconsin, Judge John C. Karel, and the Lieutenant-Governor nomination for their own Harry W. Bolens, then Mayor of Port Washington and president of the Gilson Manufacturing Company. Despite the support which some rural-based Democrats, such as Paul Husting, had lent to the tax, Karel and Bolens campaigned almost entirely on the promise of income tax repeal, usually arguing, as the manufacturers had before the legislature, that the tax would hinder the economic growth of the state.[6]

To that explicitly pro-manufacturer campaign, Francis E. McGovern, seeking re-election, responded with a sprightly defense of the income tax, buttressed by a vigorous propaganda campaign conducted by the members of the Tax Commission.[7] McGovern claimed that those fighting the income tax with the greatest tenacity—the manufacturers—were those who had the most to lose and always sought most rigorously to evade their community responsibility. The legislature had believed this too, McGovern declared, and, for that reason, had not adopted a referendum on the tax. The Governor and legislature had ignored the demands of the manufacturers because, he said, "We know the men who protested were men who were not paying their just share of the taxes in Wisconsin."[8]

The outcome of the 1912 election reinforced the progressive emphasis on the social irresponsibility of the manufacturers. Although McGovern's margin of victory was small and he lost support in traditionally progressive areas as a result of the disruptive La Follette-Roosevelt split in the Republican party, the progressives commonly believed that without the income tax issue McGovern would have lost and that, as a consequence, the outcome served to ratify the income tax.[9] Thus, no threat of repeal or significant revision emerged subsequently during McGovern's second term.

The early political isolation of the manufacturers from both progressives and other business groups emerged even more clearly during the extended reign, between 1915 and 1921, of the next Governor, conservative Emanuel L. Philipp. A superficial look at Philipp's previous political record might have led the manufacturers to expect significant support from him on their behalf. Philipp had always placed his political and business interests in close association. He owned a transportation company that supplied refrigerator cars to manufacturers, of which his best customer was the Schlitz Brewing Company; and his initial political activity, two decades earlier, had been as a Schlitz lobbyist in Washington. Success in that capacity had earned him the job of Republican Chairman of Milwaukee County in 1900.[10] Further, in 1903, Philipp had broken with La Follette, whom he had supported initially, to assist various business interests in their opposition to La Follette's program of railroad regulation. The businessmen Philipp supported included not only the brewers but the Wisconsin shippers, the paper manufacturers, small up-state manufacturers, and the manufacturers in the south who (like the brewers) relied heavily on supplies of raw materials from farmers to the north. Philipp and all of these groups believed that the existing rate

structure worked to their advantage and consequently opposed
La Follette's proposals through the vehicle of the first Wisconsin Manufacturers Association.[11]

Despite Philipp's record, his political links to the largest
Wisconsin manufacturers were, in fact, rather tenuous. In
1903–05, he had not received cooperation from the large
manufacturers, such as most of the machinery and electrical
equipment manufacturers, who had felt that they had nothing
to lose from railroad regulation. Then, in 1911, while these
same manufacturers led the attack on income taxation, Philipp
disassociated himself from that movement; Philipp's transportation interests would benefit from steeper taxation of
manufacturers, and the brewers, under mounting attack from
temperance forces, sought to avoid encouraging any further
public hostility. After 1911, Philipp adhered to the Republican
party and firmly attached himself to the fortunes of William
Howard Taft, thus increasing the distance between himself and
the largest manufacturers, who supported the more conservative Democratic organization in not only 1912 but also 1914.
As a result, when he ran for Governor, Philipp found himself
in direct opposition to the large manufacturers and, as Governor, had no obligations of any sort to the state's largest manufacturers. Further, in his 1914 campaign, Philipp had virtually
nothing to say about the income tax, thereby placing himself
clearly within the political consensus that had established the
income tax firmly in the state's fiscal system.[12]

As Governor, Philipp conciliated the more progressive
wings of the party on economic issues and moved further away
from representing directly the interests of business, especially
the manufacturers who had emerged tainted from the debacle
of 1911–12. Philipp made no more than empty gestures toward
the manufacturers and did so only when those gestures enabled
him to cater to wider interests. His hearings into the operation
of commission government, his proposal to decentralize the
Tax Commission, and his suggestion to eliminate personal
property taxation were intentionally unproductive and were
in no way designed seriously to relieve the large manufacturers.

Indeed, Philipp contributed significantly to perpetuating Wisconsin's income taxation of manufacturers, propelled by the extensive wartime use of corporate income taxation by the federal government and the esteem in which the public held income taxation, particularly that of large corporations indicted by La Follette as "war profiteers." Philipp strengthened the centralized system of tax administration and supported the movement to enact surtaxes on incomes, rather than to adopt new state mill taxes, in order to finance Wisconsin's wartime programs. The effect of these surtaxes—included in 1919 bills to finance the soldiers' bonus and educational funds—was to double corporate income tax rates in 1919, to establish a kind of excess-profits taxation, to prohibit the use of the personal property offsets against these new obligations, and to earmark all the new revenue for the state treasury. In terms of tax reform, Philipp's administration compared favorably with both that of Francis E. McGovern and that of strongly progressive John J. Blaine, who would follow Philipp in office.[13]

III

The expansion of Wisconsin income taxation during World War I represented not only an effort to punish "war profiteers" but also to enlarge the contribution of the large corporations to the state's wartime programs, particularly the funds for monetary and educational benefits for Wisconsin veterans. That interest in the revenue potential of the income tax was not new; it was an extrapolation of an interest that had developed after 1911 in using the taxation of manufacturers as a way of financing the growth of the "agricultural service-state." While the initial framers of the tax were interested only in redistributing the tax burden, once they discovered the strong buoyancy of income tax revenues they valued the tax also for the revenue bonus it provided for the state's treasury, a revenue bonus that farm progressives had begun to use on behalf of the agricultural community before they turned to financing veterans' benefits.

The development of Wisconsin's agricultural service-state, which conditioned the use of the income tax after 1911, had its roots in the pioneering efforts of the Wisconsin Dairymen's Association of William D. Hoard during the 1870's to provide small, highly specialized farmers with the ability to cope with the rigors of the competitive national marketplace. The organized dairymen promoted a program of quality control, efficiency, and the search for high-quality markets through short-course education, speakers' programs, and journalistic propaganda and invoked governmental authority to prohibit the production of low-quality dairy products damaging to the reputation of Wisconsin farmers in foreign markets.[14] It was their program of agricultural education and regulation that, when linked with the University-sponsored research and the agricultural experiment stations promoted by William A. Henry of the College of Agriculture during the 1880's, formed the kernel of the agricultural service-state.[15]

Quite distinct in purpose and character from Populist proposals to reorganize the nation's monetary and marketing systems, this program of state subsidies to promote productivity and to reach quality markets achieved early and relatively large support among Wisconsin farmers. They had clear opportunities to exploit the expansive urban market for specialized dairy products; sluggish demand for farm products conditioned their responses far less than was the case for farmers west of the Mississippi specializing in wheat and livestock production. And, when marketplace conditions became even more favorable for farmers in the first decade of the new century, the virtues of specializing in activities, such as dairying, that met the most buoyant urban demands became even more attractive. Thus, while numerous Wisconsin farmers remained hostile to scientific agriculture and many persisted in more traditional patterns of production during the "golden age" of agriculture, 1897–1913, the clientele for voluntaristic and governmental programs of regulation, research, and education expanded far beyond the farmers originally courted by William D. Hoard and William A. Henry.[16]

However, as the clientele of specialized farmers widened and as farm politics became more intense during the 1890's, the emphasis of farm reform in Wisconsin shifted from private endeavors to public initiatives. Leaders of the agricultural community reconsidered their faith in the marketplace and advocated expanding the dairy and food commission, tightening restrictions on production and marketing frauds, increasing the public investment in research and instruction, and engaging in a program to improve country roads.[17] Consequently, power passed from the agricultural associations to governmental commissions, and the College of Agriculture acquired the rudimentary extension education program of the Dairymen's Association. At the same time, the leadership of Wisconsin's specialized farmers served as one element in the political coalition that formed around Robert La Follette, William D. Hoard, and Nils P. Haugen during the 1890's to restructure state government. The espousal of the agricultural service-state was one weapon employed by the La Follette-Hoard-Haugen coalition to reduce the strength of cultural issues that divided Wisconsin's electorate. Although emphasizing a traditional Jacksonian economic morality founded upon the desirability of redistributing income through corporate tax reform, these Republicans also promoted a positive governmental order appropriate to the interests of specialized farmers within the mature industrial revolution.[18]

As a consequence of this nexus of political and economic interests and the victory of the new Republican coalition in 1900, by the time of the passage of income taxation, the costs to the state of providing educational, research, and regulatory services to agriculture had grown dramatically. In 1889, direct expenditures on the agricultural service-state (very narrowly defined) had amounted to about $62,000 and had accounted for 2.2% of total state disbursements. Their share of total disbursements was the same in 1900 but, by 1906, those expenditures had swollen to $243,000, which amounted to 4.0% of all state disbursements. These expenditures supported, for example, the dairy and food commissioner's department, the state veterinarian's department, the State Board of Agriculture, agricultural associations (such as the Wisconsin Cheesemakers' Association and the Wisconsin Dairymen's Association), agricultural experiment stations, county schools of agriculture, and county agricultural societies.[19]

By 1911, a very large segment of Wisconsin's agricultural community had developed a potent political force desiring expansion of the public services available to farmers and had led successfully a movement to institutionalize such services through governmental support. Simultaneously, an overlapping segment of the farming population, weighted more heavily toward poorer farmers, many of whom were still specializing in wheat or corn-hog production, led successfully the drive to redistribute income from manufacturing to agriculture. But those two agricultural interests were fundamentally compatible and worked in tandem, for only the manufacturers believed that such a redistributive measure would inhibit the growth of Wisconsin's marketplace—a desire of central farmers in the tradition of William D. Hoard.[20] Moreover, after 1911, as the income tax proved capable of passing a significant portion of the costs of the agricultural service-state on to the manufacturers, these two agricultural interests found their positions closely linked. After the adoption of income taxation, the state's contribution to the agricultural service-state continued to grow, reaching almost 5% of the total state disbursements by 1918. Between 1912 and 1918, such expenditures increased from $338,000 to $822,000 or by a net of $484,000. Also, between 1912 and 1918, the net increase in state revenues provided by the income tax (subtracting the revenues returned to county and municipal governments and the costs of administering the Tax Commission) came to $441,000, thus nearly matching the increase in expenditure.[21] To the Wisconsin manufacturer, the expansion of the agricultural service state simply worsened the impact of the income tax system. In response, the more politically enlightened manufacturers encouraged and supported voluntaristic approaches to the marketplace problems of the farmers to reduce support for costly government programs.[22]

The dynamic revenue-producing capacity of the income tax during a period of buoyant income, which surprised supporters of the original measure, contributed to the movement to extend income taxation thereafter. The wartime emergency forced the state to seek new revenues and brought fruition to the growing desires of more radical progressives to tie income tax increases to the funding of specific state programs. The more conservative farm progressives opposed creating such connections. They were persuaded by the arguments of Governor Emanuel L. Philipp that surtaxes on corporations would be an unreliable means of providing consistent levels of support for most state institutions, such as the University, and might well subject those institutions to corporate domination.[23] Moreover, those same progressives, usually the more prosperous, were concerned about the impact of uniformly higher income tax rates on their own profits. Consequently, they weakened progressive support during and after World War I for surtaxes and increased rates.[24] Yet these same more-conservative progressives favored expanding the income taxation of corporations through the repeal of the property tax offset and enlarging the share of income tax revenues taken by the state government for its own purposes. Both conservative and more radical farm progressives agreed on the rectitude of the new income tax thrust that began in World War I and was carried forward in the 1920's; they valued expansion of the tax to both redistribute income and expand the agricultural service-state.

The income tax system of 1911 had not only provided new state revenues but allowed expansion of state aids and generated revenues distributed directly to counties and municipalities. Such funds permitted property tax relief, particularly for farmers; at the same time, they created the basis for some improvement of public facilities, especially country roads and rural schools. By World War I, all rural progressives had come to agree on the desirability of enhancing the resources available on the countryside for farm property tax relief and the financing of the basic services of transportation and education; they applauded the success of the income tax in successfully doing just that.[25] However, in the agricultural crisis during the 1920–21 depression, the system of distribution established in 1911 did not suffice to meet the needs of the large population stranded in the "cut-over" district of Wisconsin's northern counties. The massive migration of farmers taking up new land in the northern counties had reached its peak during the inflationary boom induced by World War I. The following collapse of farm prices exposed the weak economic base of the area and brought about falling property valuations, delinquent taxes, and an inability of that new population to satisfy its taste for public services, particularly elementary schools and good roads. Recognizing the strength of that segment in the progressive coalition, and still hoping for successful economic development of the region along agricultural lines, the state, in the 1920's, embarked upon a program of increasing state aids for schools and highways that was directed at low-income counties, mainly in the "cut-over" district. This political pressure for expanded state aids to poorer areas or for the redistribution of income to less successful agricultural enterprise became part of the force to expand income taxation and contributed to the 1925 reforms. And those reforms permitted a substantial growth in state tax revenues during the rest of the decade which, in turn facilitated an expanded program of state aids.[26]

From the standpoint of the manufacturers, this revenue redirection worsened even further the competitive disadvantages wrought by the Wisconsin tax system for, in addition to increasing the cost of capital, it shifted revenues that might have been devoted to urban districts to rural areas. Ultimately, during the additional stress caused by the Great Depression, the enormity of the misallocation of resources inherent in large urban-subsidies to northern Wisconsin became all too clear. The burden of state aids provided for northern counties led the state to induce the counties to zone themselves to establish a more efficient agriculture, to promote the relocation of excess farmers (with the assistance of New Deal resettlement funds), and to establish an effective forest conservation program. Only then did progressives recognize the logic of the marketplace sufficiently to plan for the integration of the North in the economic development of the state.[27] Although the culmination of the story of the "cut-over" was one of success in regional planning, it came too late to prevent significant retardation in the growth of manufacturing activity in Wisconsin.

IV

The agricultural crisis of the early 1920's provided an opportunity for the reform-minded wing of the Republican party to restore the unquestioned primacy of economic issues over the cultural issues that the social tensions of World War I had exaggerated in Wisconsin. Reaffirming the appeal of a secular pietism, the progressive leadership developed a message that was more heatedly anticorporate in tone than at any time since 1912. In his 1920 gubernatorial campaign, progressive John J. Blaine developed a set of close associations with the radical wing of Wisconsin's farmers, which had gathered strength during World War I, well before the agricultural reversals of the 1920–21 depression. A more radical farm politics, reminiscent of the Populism of the Plains states, had already appeared in the campaign which the candidate of the Wisconsin Society of Equity, James Tittemore, waged for the Governor's chair in 1918. Yet a significant number of Wisconsin farmers had found even Tittemore insufficiently radical; by the beginning of 1920, the Nonpartisan League of North Dakota had attracted over 20,000 farmers in Wisconsin to membership. When Tittemore and the more conservative Equity members refused to embrace the League, Blaine capitalized on the obvious opportunity and accepted the League's endorsement for Governor. Moreover, he explicitly supported the League's platform and campaigned with three

League representatives on his state ticket. The result was an electoral victory in 1920 that owed less to Wisconsin's urban population than had any previous progressive victory.[28]

A desire to restructure the market for agricultural goods was important to the redirection of farmer politics, but at the heart of Blaine's political message was an old-fashioned tax threat to the state's manufacturing corporations. As the important Blaine supporter and later Tax Commissioner Charles Rosa put it: "The big fellows, the profiteers, the tax dodgers, and the seeker after special privilege will find consideration at his (Blaine's) hands but it will not be the thing they are looking for."[29] Blaine intensified his attack on manufacturers as enormous "tax dodgers" during his first term in office and, in 1922, won re-election even more handily.[30] After 1922, Blaine and the progressive proponents of redistributing the tax burden away from farmers argued that the marketplace and the tax system both failed to reflect what urbanites owed farmers. To buttress Blaine's judgment that the state should divert income from cities and manufacturers to rural areas, Rosa asserted that "There could be no packers income without hogs—no shoe manufacturers income without hides—no wholesalers, jobbers or retailers income without the people who live often far beyond the confines of the city in which the income is accumulated and taxed." Equally reminiscent of the Populist enthusiasms of the 1890's, another radical progressive argued that cities grew and prospered at the expense of the countryside: "Wealth grows within the city walls," he declared, "only because the city robs the farm." Conjuring up the well-worn romantic image of the city as monster, he asserted that "The thrust of the city's tentacles extends into every nook and corner of the state."[31]

Thus, in their new campaign, the income tax proponents went to brink of an explicitly anti-industrial ideology for the first time in Wisconsin's income tax movement. The depths of the agricultural crisis during the early 1920's lent an unusual popularity to anti-industrial persuasions in the depressed areas of northern Wisconsin. Nonetheless, in drafting tax policy, progressive politicians continued to recognize the desirability of concern for Wisconsin's industrial opportunities. Governor Blaine and legislative leaders sought reassurance from Tax Commission, Legislative Reference Library, and University of Wisconsin experts on the likely impact of changes in tax policy on industrial expansion. But, as had been the case for more than a decade, expert and progressive politician alike lent no serious intellectual consideration to the marketplace issues raised by the manufacturers. Not only did progressives brush off the economic arguments of the manufacturers but they ignored the obvious fact that the income tax movement elsewhere in industrial states had lost all momentum with the end of the fiscal demands of World War I. Even if it had been easy to believe in the pedagogical power of Wisconsin's tax policies in 1911, by the early 1920's it should have been absolutely apparent that other industrial states and the federal government were committed to policies more favorable to large manufacturing corporations.[32]

Ignoring the arguments of the manufacturers and without developing any reservations with regard to limiting industrial growth, progressives intensified their long-standing efforts to redistribute income toward agriculture and to enhance the agricultural service-state. They concentrated upon two specific reforms: (1) the diversion of more income tax revenues to state government and (2) the repeal of the personal property tax offset. The former would provide for enlarged state aids to and property tax relief for the poorer agricultural districts, and the latter would nearly double income tax revenues and shift state taxes toward the corporations that accounted for the vast majority of the funds lost to the state as a result of the offset. At the same time, offset repeal would not increase the tax burdens on farmers.[33] While the offset repeal encountered some opposition from the relatively prosperous Wisconsin farmers, it gained compensating support from the Socialists, and legislative success for the offset appeared feasible as early as the legislative session of 1923.[34] However, Socialists and urban progressives disagreed strenuously with any redistribution of income tax revenues that would favor the state at the expense of the cities. Their opposition to that part of the radical farmer program led them to hold up formation of a tax reform package until the next session.[35] By 1925, however, the farm progressives had gained sufficient support to enact not only offset repeal but a sharp increase in the state's share of income tax revenues from 10% to 50%.[36] Following the 1925 act, using the new income tax revenues, the state dramatically increased its level of state subsidies, particularly subventions for depressed northern Wisconsin.

V

When Emanuel L. Philipp was in the Governor's chair (1915–1921), the Wisconsin manufacturers tended to abandon special organization as a means of coping with legislative and electoral tax politics. When politically active manufacturers, such as Otto Falk, had a case to make for decentralized commission administration or against surtaxes, they tended to prefer to take their propositions personally and individually to a Governor who was cordial and sympathetic, although not an intimate ally. As a result of the attractiveness of cultivating personal ties with the Governor, the WMA became relatively quiescent, the MMMA limited itself usually to strictly Milwaukee issues, and the large manufacturers abandoned the Democratic party as a convenient vehicle for changing the direction of state-level taxation. But, by 1923, the revival of old-style class politics in Wisconsin led to a resumption of organized efforts, including public affirmation by the manufacturers of their contribution to the economic order and their high level of social responsibility.

The renewed organized responses of the manufacturers proved, however, to be once again characterized by unbending rigidity. They chose to engage in all-out opposition to progressive measures that threatened larger tax levies, to deny that there were acceptable alternatives to the maintenance of the *status quo* or some form of tax relief for themselves, and to believe in their ability to arouse public fears of retarded economic growth. But that was not because the manufacturers had failed to contemplate other courses of action. In particular, in 1923, two successful politicians, ex-Governor Philipp and Lawrence C. Whittet, former Speaker of the Assembly, attempted to bring a new kind of leadership to Wisconsin's largest corporations. Concerned about the radical direction taken by progressives and the administration of John J. Blaine, they took charge of the Milwaukee Association of Commerce (the MMMA until 1917) to provide a more effective management of the political affairs of the manufacturers.[37] Although Philipp agreed (in private) that the 1923 tax bills "read as though there is an intention of persecuting business" and that the present group of progressives were "the product of twenty years of agitation" and were "of the radical type," he argued that the manufacturers should seek openings to the progressives and encourage farmers to seek voluntaristic solutions to their problems. Not only would cooperation yield areas of compromise but compromise would avoid worsening Wisconsin's growing reputation of a "high-tax" state. He argued that if higher taxes became a reality, it would be even more important to attract new industry in order to distribute more widely the burden of the agricultural service-state carried by manufacturers.[38]

Building from the MAC, Philipp and Whittet tried to form a State Development Committee and then a Greater Wisconsin Association, but the largest manufacturers, both within and without Milwaukee, proved either unwilling to engage in any form of cooperative enterprise or, more commonly, strongly committed already to the more rigid approach of the WMA. Many of the latter were indifferent to the blandishments of Philipp, who they felt had been a grim disappointment as Governor.[39] (The former group consisted mainly of the brewing interests, Philipp's natural constituency among manufacturers and also a group embittered over the support that other manufacturers had given to the Wisconsin Anti-Saloon League.[40])

Thus, in 1923 the WMA directed the political energies of the largest manufacturers and, consequently, virtually no interest in a compromise with the progressives surfaced. The WMA failed to play on the divisions of issue and personality among farm spokesmen, urban progressives, and Socialists, despite Blaine's hint of a desire to make a limited deal with Senate conservatives.[41] Certainly, given the combined strength of radical progressives in the legislature, the manufacturers had little room to maneuver in 1923. Nonetheless, a compromise would have very likely prevented the stalemate that helped to stoke up progressive fires in the 1924 legislative and gubernatorial campaigns that returned a legislature and governor even less interested in barters with the manufacturers.[42] The manufacturers had relinquished their most promising opening to stave off the blows the progressives administered in 1925.

After the stand-off of 1923 and before the decisive legislative session of 1925, the WMA revived its policy of taking the manufacturers' case to the public and, in so doing, portraying the Wisconsin tax system in the most unfavorable light possible. In the winter of 1923–24, to equip the manufacturers with more effective arguments, the WMA financed the National Industrial Conference Board in a study of tax conditions in Wisconsin.[43] That report, by Laurence R. Gottlieb, a New York University economist, appeared in August of 1924.[44] Although the report served to enhance the intellectual substance of the manufacturers' position, it contributed to the mobilization of public opinion against the manufacturers and, just as Philipp and Whittet predicted, served to worsen seriously Wisconsin's national reputation as an investment site.[45]

Politically more significant than the Gottlieb report was the launching of an extensive publicity campaign, financed by manufacturer contributions and including twenty advertisements placed throughout the state's press by the WMA, that dwelt upon the role of the manufacturers in the Wisconsin community.[46] Although the campaign was one segment of a larger, nationwide public relations effort of business during the

1920's, the state program differed from the national enterprise by articulating a rather clear, market-oriented social philosophy and by having undesirable political results from the point of view of the manufacturers.[47]

It was a campaign based on the manufacturers' complete distrust of Wisconsin's politicians, mirroring the progressives' own concept of the manufacturers. For example, privately W. H. Alford, vice-president of Nash Motors in Kenosha and a WMA leader, described the Wisconsin political leadership as composed of "cheap politicians, who pay no taxes, who have never done anything for the upbuilding of the state, but have spent their time in trying to inflame the mass of our citizens against those who furnish employment to thousands of working people in the state and pay out millions of dollars in wages."[48] By way of contrast, the largest manufacturers explicitly identified themselves to the public and declared themselves to be "men whose reputation for honesty and fair dealing is above reproach, men who have done much to the advancement of industry in the state of Wisconsin and to the upbuilding of the communities in which they live."[49] They expressed confidence that the "rank and file of Wisconsin citizens" respected their judgment and would heed their appeal for "a rational public sentiment," as Walter J. Kohler described the publicity campaign.[50]

To underscore their social responsibility, the manufacturers asserted the unity of interests between agriculture and manufacturing; they harkened back to the rhetoric of community builders in the nineteenth century who had promoted domestic industries to complement the growth of specialized agriculture. The farm and factory reinforced each other in that "the best markets for the farm are where the most factories are"—witness the higher prices for milk which dairy farmers in Milwaukee and Kenosha counties received in contrast with farmers to the north—and "the best factory markets are where the farmers are the most prosperous." They used rhetoric reminiscent of the days of Populism and, earlier and more pertinent to Wisconsin experience, the Wisconsin Dairymen's Association, to proclaim the unity of producers and the dependence of consumers on their activities. Doctors, lawyers, and merchants owed "their livelihood to production, their prosperity and opportunity to Farm and Factory." But the manufacturers' concept of the community and their appropriate social role did not depart from the norms of the marketplace. At the same time that the manufacturers stressed the communal unity of the state's economic interests and avowed a sense of obligation for the prosperity of that community, they also declared that they would not hesitate to take the most rational economic course, regardless of the interests of the wider society as determined by the political process. Agreeing with the progressives that they would have to pay the tax increases out of profits, given their inability to pass on the tax on the short run, the manufacturers threatened the community with the consequent loss of new investment and a significant retardation of income and employment.[51] Thus, in their conception of their social role, the Wisconsin manufacturers adhered to the narrow road of profit maximization; on the one hand, the manufacturers maintained that their fundamental mission was to increase the prosperity of the community at large but, on the other hand, they declared that their sole guide in social behavior was "market" rigor.[52]

The propagandizing by the manufacturers did, in fact, include a reasonably accurate representation of economic reality, but their political effort served mainly to clarify the progressive cast of the issues and to facilitate the adoptions of the controversial tax measures. To much of the Wisconsin public, including the tax experts who served the state, examples of corporate opposition to tax reform were simply instances of efforts to dodge communal responsibility.[53] Widening the public's exposure to the tax issue in 1924–25 only increased public support for imposing a larger tax burden on the manufacturing corporations. When the outcome of the 1925 legislative session had become all too clear, the leaders of the WMA finally realized that their energies had been misdirected.[54] W. H. Alford confessed that their campaign had been "looked upon with suspicion" by the "Wisconsin citizenry."[55] His belated insight found ample confirmation in the complete ineffectiveness of the manufacturers in bending the 1925 legislature.

The political defeat of 1925 was so decisive that it purged the manufacturers of their self-righteous pretensions and led them to become disposed toward accepting the practicality of the Philipp approach to politics. Fortuitously, they almost simultaneously found an appropriate opening. A vicious internal struggle for the leadership of the Wisconsin Republican party, touched off by the 1925 death of Robert M. La Follette, Sr., provided the manufacturers with an opportunity to exploit divisions among progressives. In the gubernatorial campaign of 1926, the manufacturers turned from their support of the highly conservative, traditionalist wing of the party, led by a group of Oshkosh Republicans who sought to elect their own candidate, to advance the candidacy of Secretary of State Fred H. Zimmerman of Milwaukee, who found support from urban progressives, prosperous farmers, and even some rural proponents of radical tax reform.[56]

W. H. Alford of Nash financed the Zimmerman campaign and other manufacturers—Otto Falk and George Kull as the Secretary of the WMA, in particular—spread the word among the manufacturing community that the conservative candidate, although ideologically preferable, could not be elected and that Zimmerman was the lesser of two evils.[57] Moreover, these manufacturers cautiously avoided the kind of public commitment that had characterized their earlier political plunges. The manufacturers responded much differently to the established fact of income taxation than they had previously. Instead of blindly seeking virtually complete repeal of the corporate legislation, they declared their willingness to accept alternative measures. Although their new proposals were not major concessions in 1926, they were indicative of the new mood of the manufacturers and improved their public posture.[58] With the financial support of the largest manufacturers and the electoral support from progressives dissenting from the claim of Robert M. La Follette, Jr., to party leadership,

Zimmerman defeated handily the "La Follette" candidate, Herman Ekern, in the primary and then went on to win even more easily in November, 1926.

The change in strategy and Zimmerman's victory provided the manufacturers, for the first time, with a degree of protection from further fiscal attack by powerful agricultural interests supported by nonmanufacturing corporations. Farm progressives in the legislature were able to carry measures to toughen further the administration of the law and succeeded in defeating a series of tax proposals sponsored by both conservatives and urban progressives. But they could not further increase the tax rates and, in fact, suffered a defeat in 1927 when Zimmerman and few progressive Senators paid off political obligations by an act enabling corporations to average incomes over three years in calculating taxable income. Although the act was defended accurately in theory as a measure that would allow corporations to take account of "loss" years, in practice, during a period of generally buoyant prices, it had the effect of reducing most corporate income tax bills.[59] That concession to the manufacturers, however, resulted in Zimmerman's political demise. A quirk in the averaging measure, forcing the state to collect only back and delinquent taxes in fiscal 1928, meant that Zimmerman had to sponsor an increase in the state's general property tax levy. That widely unpopular act, coupled with the continuing division among progressives, contributed to Zimmerman's defeat for re-election. However, Zimmerman's support for the manufacturers had been indirect enough not to taint him, and his successor as Governor turned out to be Walter J. Kohler, the manufacturer of bathroom fixtures, who would acquire a national reputation as an exponent of narrow business-paternalism.[60]

The election of 1928 marked a reunion of the conservative Oshkosh Republican organization and the large manufacturers behind a single candidate but, given the persistence of the WMA in maintaining low political visibility, Kohler was free to draw support from a wide enough sector of the population to carry the state against two other candidates, Joseph D. Beck and the hapless Zimmerman, who split the progressive vote between them. Like Emanuel Philipp, Kohler engineered his own campaign, developing a personal following and avoiding identification with prominent conservatives. Partly because of the interests he represented directly, he was more successful than Philipp in forming a buffer between the manufacturing interests and any new initiatives in the taxation of corporations. Although Kohler was unable and unwilling, given the residual any of the progressive legislation, he vetoed a 1929 measure to both increase income tax rates and repeal the income-averaging provision. Moreover, he encouraged the continued growth of the political power of manufacturers in Wisconsin by supporting the placement of aluminum manufacturer George Vits on the Republican National Committee and by granting Vits single-handed control of federal patronage in Wisconsin. But Kohler's political fortunes and the placid period for the manufacturers would both end as the Great Depression intervened, returning the state to an earlier political pattern by uniting progressives and bringing another La Follette to the Governorship.[61]

Thus, on the eve of the Depression, the manufacturers, reinforced by progressive divisiveness, had contributed to the stabilizing of political conditions affecting their capital markets. The basic support for progressivism remained, however, and precluded any attempt to recast the administration of the tax or enact tax reductions. Thus, even when the manufacturers had apparently succeeded in extending the economic "normalcy" of Harding-Coolidge to Wisconsin, they were faced with the continuing political necessity of accepting the reality of Wisconsin's progressive state. The manufacturers had learned they had opportunities for compromise that were well worth taking but, at the same time, they had discovered once again the impact on tax policy of the fundamental distribution of political power in Wisconsin.

5

WISCONSIN'S PROGRESSIVE POLITICAL ECONOMY: AN OVERVIEW

I

The Wisconsin income tax likely prevented the state from making the most of her growth opportunities. If we accept certain assumptions about business behavior, especially the eminently plausible premise that firms sought to maximize profits, then we are led to the conclusion that the income tax retarded capital formation in the manufacturing sector. Indications of the extent of the impact of this retardation on economic growth are plain, even without measurement of the precise influence. The state's pace of manufacturing development fell behind that for its region as a whole during the critical period between 1909 and 1929. In the light of the centrality of manufacturing expansion to the process of economic growth during the period, the importance of manufacturing to the Great Lakes during the period, and Wisconsin's locational situation, the pattern implies that the income tax had an acute inhibiting influence on Wisconsin's growth.

Although the Wisconsin income taxes applied to manufacturing profits were not exceptionally high by the standards set by the post-New Deal federal tax, during the period from 1911 to 1929 they were high by standards prevailing throughout the nation and, significantly, were the only such taxes adopted in the Great Lakes states. Moreover, as Wisconsin did not allow a compensating reduction in property taxation, the interaction between Wisconsin's income and property tax systems resulted in significantly larger burdens of property taxation than those borne by manufacturers elsewhere in the Great Lakes region. If Wisconsin had allowed the differentials in the cost of capital resulting from income taxation to prevail for only a brief period, their impact on economic growth would have been minimal. But the state maintained those differentials for two decades and, in addition, fostered political movements that first threatened and then actually imposed further increases in taxation of the incomes and property of manufacturers. Not only did the capital-cost differentials persist for an extended period, but that period consisted of the most crucial 20 years in the industrialization of the Great Lakes States. The combination of the capital-cost disadvantage, the sustained period over which the disadvantage prevailed, and the central role of that period in the era of mature industrial revolution disappointed the aspirations of Wisconsin's citizenry, both businessmen and the progressive antagonists of the manufacturers, for maximizing the state's chances for rapid economic growth.

II

The deleterious impact of the income tax was rooted in the absence of close political relationships between progressives and the larger manufacturers. Although manufacturers and powerful politicians found areas for extensive cooperation in more industrial states and on the federal level, in Wisconsin they were at loggerheads over taxation continuously after 1909. From that sharp quarrel, the manufacturers emerged as the political losers. The manufacturers bore the brunt of the expansion of income taxation and the associated increases in property taxation. Even during their brief episode of political success in the late 1920's, the larger Wisconsin manufacturers found themselves contending with a public that valued the income tax, particularly its corporate provisions, for its two-pronged conformity to nineteenth-century ideals of equality of taxation and its ability to transfer resources from manufacturing into agriculture. Accordingly, the large manufacturers encountered a distribution of political power that reinforced the structure of the economy by tending to support the interests of agriculture and Wisconsin's utility corporations at the expense of the manufacturing sector.

The timing of the movement to tax the manufacturers should be explained partially in terms of the heady anticorporate passions inflamed by the economic and political turmoil of the 1890's. Those passions focused on the issues of taxation and the social irresponsibility of corporations. In addition, in the 1890's and the following decade, the growing national awareness of the rise of the corporate-manufacturing sector of the economy that created new assets not reached by the general property tax advanced the interest in tax reform. But that interest focused on income taxation only where a fundamental political condition prevailed: the relative strength of agricultural interests. In Wisconsin, the agricultural sector was relatively large, the manufacturing sector relatively small, and, during the 1890's, the Republican party leadership proved adept in facilitating a widened and deepened participation of farmers in politics, thereby heightening political cleavages along economic lines. In this sense, Wisconsin progressivism was both a mass and a class movement as well as the working-out of interest group pressures.[1] Thus, the politics of Wisconsin taxation ought to be interpreted primarily in terms of the way in which the distribution of political power reflected the structure of the economy and the relative scale of manufacturing units.

This interpretation of progressive politics, based on the development of tax policy, should be consistent with the politics of other progressive policy directions aimed at altering the behavior of manufacturers. Although the focus of this study has been taxation and rigorous analysis of the impact of other progressive policies remains to be performed, consistency seems to prevail. These regulatory measures, passed largely during the critical 1911 legislative session, included the regulation of the wages, hours, and working conditions of women, the regulation of child labor, the creation of the Industrial Commission to enforce labor regulations, and the enactment of workmen's accident compensation. The passage of these measures did represent, in part, the vigorous efforts of urban progressives and Social Democrats. But the easy passage of this body of legislation, particularly the regulation of the labor of women, which offered the prospect of higher wage rates, like taxation suggests the relative political weakness of the manufacturers.[2] Further, the ease of passage also illustrates the power of agricultural interests, for only their support was necessary for the expeditious enactment of such measures. They were interested in supporting campaign promises made to enhance the appeal of the Republican party in urban centers, they recognized that these measures would pose no costs to the farming community, and in 1911 they were highly receptive to antimanufacturer legislation.[3] Moreover, these initiatives passed only because dominant rural and small-town progressives felt they had nothing to lose economically and something to gain politically. Whenever urban social-justice legislation happened to pose significant costs to Wisconsin farmers, progressives buried those proposals. Most notably, during the 1920's, the fears of rural progressives that they would have to shoulder a significant portion of the costs of unemployment relief consistently defeated a program of unemployment compensation.[4] In addition, farm progressives appear to have been unwilling to fund adequately the enforcement machinery for labor legislation created in the Industrial Commission.[5] In contrast, farm progressives were willing to pass on the costs of relief for distressed farmers to urbanites and provided consistently vigorous support for the income tax assessment work of the Tax Commission. It is reasonable to suggest that, in Wisconsin, labor legislation played a lesser role in the development of the progressive state than policies of taxation, but both revealed the same distribution of political power.

An interpretation of the development of Wisconsin's political culture relying on the structure of the economy provides an explanation for the earlier and more sustained occurrence of progressive efforts to redistribute income from manufacturers in Wisconsin, the tendency of other income tax states to protect manufacturing profits, and the policy of the federal government during the 1920's to reduce the income taxation of manufacturers. With that association between political power and economic structure in mind, it is far easier to reconcile the more radical character of the Wisconsin progressive movement with the more conservative direction of progressivism in other industrial states and at the federal level.[6]

An alternative interpretation of state-level progressivism that focuses on the urban social-justice characteristics of the expansion of government during the period is also based on the relative timing of progressive legislation designed to regulate and tax manufacturers.[7] That view holds that the adoption of structural reforms in the economy occurred in Wisconsin and California before New York and Massachusetts because of the differences in the social behavior of manufacturers. According to this view, in the East, businessmen developed private means for ameliorating the social ills of industrialization. However, as in the newer western states the need for public action in easing the social adjustment to modern, industrial-urban society was greater, a smaller gap existed between the creation of social problems associated with industrialization and the extension of government activity to those problems than in the older eastern states.

Although that interpretation is stimulating, it does not reveal the core of Wisconsin progressivism. It is true that Wisconsin manufacturers, proud of their reputations as nineteenth-century community builders, were powerfully committed to profit maximization as the optimal criterion for their social behavior and, without doubt, that disposition antagonized and created political opportunities for Wisconsin progressives.[8] Further, such an interpretation may explain the relative timing of Wisconsin's 1911 labor legislation. But that legislation was central to neither progressive politics nor the progressive state in Wisconsin. Of far more significance than labor legislation was Wisconsin tax policy and, insofar as taxation was concerned, the Wisconsin progressive movement was not an effort to account for the costs of industrialization-urbanization but thrusts to redistribute income in favor of agriculture and to create the agricultural service state. Wisconsin progressivism appears to have been more a response to the configuration of competing economic and political interests with a heavily agricultural flavor than an impulse toward industrial democracy.

It is evident that progressives, despite their extreme tax position, were not simply camouflaged Populists. Although they framed the income tax initially in the romantic spirit of the restoration of nineteenth-century "equality" of taxation and also for the hard-headed purpose of redistributing income from manufacturing corporations to farmers, their objectives soon became more complex and more responsive to the needs of farmers in an industrial society. In 1911, the progressives had strong doubts about the revenue potential of the income tax because the problems of administering an income tax appeared so formidable. But the Wisconsin tax experts, applying themselves with devotion to those knotty problems of administration, quickly demonstrated the capacity of an income tax to augment general revenues in a period of economic expansion. Thereafter, progressives sought to use the tax not simply as a means of "equalizing revenues" but as a central way to finance a rapid expansion of the agricultural service-state. The set of services devised was rationally designed to equip small farmers with an enhanced ability to compete in the national marketplace.

Despite their modern institutional reforms, the progressives chose a method of financing the new costs of government that the Populists might well have applauded: they simply passed the costs on to the politically weaker manufacturing community. In effect, the farm progressives were concerned both with the issues of wealth redistribution and with issues surrounding the creation of the modern service-regulatory state. Wisconsin progressives, in contrast with those in New York and Massachusetts, emphasized redistribution by passing a sharply restrictive income tax with respect to the manufacturers and merged the two objectives by using the income tax as a source of revenue for the agricultural service-state. The Wisconsin version of progressivism was highly responsive to "industrial" agriculture but negligent of the interests of manufacturers and, consequently, of the economy as a whole. Thus, Wisconsin's "broker" state meant the firmer entrenchment of the interests of agriculture in the political order. As elsewhere in the nation, progressivism was open to influence from widely diverse economic interests, but weighted toward the more powerful economic groups. But, in distinction from the typical pattern in older industrial states, the manufacturers found themselves poorly represented in the "broker" state.

Earlier, western states encouraged the location of manufacturing within their borders.[9] That favorable attitude toward manufacturing development very likely provided a shield for the manufacturing corporations during the 1890's when Wisconsin politicians, both rural and urban, began to fasten their attention upon the taxation and regulation of utilities. Also, in the 1890's, manufacturing corporations were protected by the fact that, having only recently begun reorganization on a large-scale basis, they were less visible as immediate targets for equalitarian anticorporatism than the more established large utility corporations, particularly the railroads. But at an early point the utilities significantly moderated their tax burden, in contrast with the manufacturers' long record of defeat. The explanation rests, more importantly, in a distribution of corporate political power in Wisconsin that favored the utilities. But that explanation leaves unresolved the significance of progressive attitudes toward the contribution of manufacturing to economic growth. At no point did the progressives explicitly reject the nineteenth-century town promoters' attachment to the desirability of manufacturing. Even the neo-Populist rhetorical excesses of the early 1920's were outweighed by continuing progressive recognition of the value of high-productivity manufacturing employment. However, those who shaped Wisconsin's political order in the first decades of the century had adopted a new view of what was necessary to maintain a healthy manufacturing sector. In particular, they accepted the advice extended to them by Wisconsin's tax experts that they were not retarding economic growth through their special taxation of manufacturing assets and incomes. Such advice was precisely what the Wisconsin progressives, concerned with redistributing the costs of government and keeping down the expense of government to agricultural interests, wished to hear.

A superficially attractive apology for the Wisconsin experts is that they believed other states would follow Wisconsin's good example in taxing manufacturing profits at higher rates and thus alleviate any competitive disadvantage befalling Wisconsin in the short run. If the excuse were valid, one would fault the tax experts primarily for their poor political judgment. However, Wisconsin tax experts virtually never expressed a belief in the likelihood of other states developing rigorous systems of corporate income and property taxation. Their consistent advice was to ignore whatever differentials in corporate taxation existed between Wisconsin and her neighboring states. By underestimating the significance of interstate differentials in the taxation of manufacturing capital, the experts failed to recognize that in an expansive, well-integrated economy organized under a federal political system, taxation of the profits of large corporations is implemented best, from the standpoint of optimal national regional development, by the national government.

In conclusion, the progressive redistributive criterion should be viewed as incompatible with their objective of economic growth. In that sense, progressive tax policy was irrational. But the source of that irrationality was not simply the moralism of the progressive world view; the opponents of the progressives, particularly the manufacturers, shrouded their own position in a communal morality of at least equal intensity. Instead, the element of irrationality stemmed from the substantive content of that progressive moralism or the strength of an attachment to an impractical pre-industrial ideal of tax equity, which, in turn, was the almost inevitable expression of a set of narrowly defined class interests.

III

Just as the structure of the economy can help explain the contours of tax policy and progressivism in Wisconsin, it can provide an understanding of the political behavior of Wisconsin manufacturers in coping with progressive tax policy. The most suggestive facts are the relatively small size of the Wisconsin manufacturing sector and the small scale of even the largest Wisconsin manufacturers. Also, while the full history of the structure of Wisconsin business remains unwritten, it appears likely that during the period an unusually high share of Wisconsin manufacturing corporations was owned by Wisconsin families and that, far more than in the largest industrial states of the Great Lakes, manufacturing activity in Wisconsin was conducted in cities of relatively small size.[10] All these factors, joined with a relatively recent history of nineteenth-century town building, created a community of manufacturers of strikingly narrow social vision, one that included no calculus other than that of the marketplace. For almost all the leaders of the Wisconsin manufacturing community, including those based in Milwaukee, the tax policies of the progressives seemed not only unprecedented, given the nineteenth-century emphasis on the encouragement of manufacturing, but so obnoxious to their concept of an orderly community that they often refused to recognize the strength of their political opposition as well as its social legitimacy. The progressives had no monopoly on moralistic rhetoric and, if anything, had a firmer grip on political reality.

Until manufacturers had absorbed the lesson of 1925 in politics, the only manufacturers who sought accommodation with reform forces, and thereby conformed to the typical pattern of manufacturer behavior in older industrial states, were the very few, like Emanuel E. Philipp, who had personal experience and familiarity with the character of regulation-taxation within modern society. Manufacturers were rarely willing to make compromises with the progressives and persisted in explaining their opposition to higher taxes with a highly paternalistic social philosophy. The manufacturers usually denied the propriety of making "sliding-scale" contributions to government, as the progressives demanded; consequently, they simply confirmed their popular image as "tax-dodgers," lacking in community responsibility. At the same time, they created greater opportunities for political leaders to press forward anticorporate platforms. Only late in the 1920's, after continued political reversals, did manufacturers like W. H. Alvord, George Vits, and Walter J. Kohler begin to take advantage of the most realistic opportunities. The result was a brief period of political stability before the Great Depression, although manufacturers were never in a position to undo the progressive state. Thus, although the large manufacturers faced a distribution of political power and a conceptualization of the issues unfavorable to their interests, their political difficulties also resulted from their faulty social vision and their consequent political ineptitude.

In contrast, Wisconsin's older corporations, such as the railroads, had learned to cope with anticorporate passions and had accepted the necessity of working within the framework of the communal order defined by progressives. As a result of this, as well as their fundamentally greater political weight, these corporations were able to blunt the political force of progressivism and move political competition for economic rewards solely within the realm of interest-group competition. In the process, they implicitly accepted the belief that the public interest would be served best by a pragmatic, multilateral willingness to compromise. The manufacturers, however, with few exceptions, found it difficult to accept that pluralist notion. True, Wisconsin's pluralist development, insofar as the manufacturers were concerned, was incomplete; the oppor-

tunities for profitable compromise were relatively few. But, by
failing to take advantage of those that were available, as the
railroads had done, they closed avenues for expanding those
opportunities that would have been available in an atmosphere
of greater trust.

IV

The progressives as well as the large manufacturers favored rapid economic growth for Wisconsin. But the progressives centered less on providing the political framework most
favorable to growth in the context of an integrated national
economy and more on supporting agriculture and working
out in practice their nineteenth-century notions of tax equality. The progressives wanted economic and industrial growth,
but on terms they themselves would set through the political
process. The manufacturers, for their part, denied any responsibility to social considerations external to the marketplace.
The large manufacturers, however, were the ones in the position to make the most important developmental decisions.
Their political isolation very likely retarded economic growth.
The Wisconsin progressive movement was flawed most significantly in that the progressives, in their effort to maximize
economic opportunity, failed to include all those sectors with
crucial economic power. Accepting as they did the nation's
fundamental legal framework reinforcing the reign of a capitalist order, the progressives erred in failing to account for
the interests of perhaps the most important sector of capitalists in framing their tax legislation. Although cast in terms
of the enlightened search for economic democracy within a
capitalist system, the Wisconsin reform movement was an
expression of the shortsighted self-interest of a politically
powerful sector of the economy.

APPENDIX: THE CAPITAL-COSTS TEST

The Measure. The development of a measure for the true resource cost of using capital—the user cost, or rental price, or shadow price of capital—was founded upon a model based on an assumption that manufacturers battle to maximize their net worth by maximizing net revenues after taxes. Alternatively, one could assume that manufacturers sought to minimize the discounted value of their contractual outlays, i.e., those of labor, capital, and taxes, taking output, the price of output, and the production function as given.[1] Whichever approach is followed, maximization or minimization, the result is the now familiar user cost of capital modified by a set of tax conditions or parameters. That basic user cost, without the tax modifications, is:

$$C = q(r + \delta)$$

where c is the user cost of capital, q the price of capital goods, r the prevailing interest rate, and δ is the real rate of depreciation. Making the most fundamental adjustments for income and property tax variables yields the following expression for user costs:[2]

$$C = q\left[\frac{1-uv}{1-u}\delta + \frac{1-uw}{1-u}r + \frac{1-uy}{1-u}\rho\right]$$

where ρ is the rate of property taxation, u the rate of income taxation, and v, w, and y are the proportions of depreciation, interest, and property taxes, respectively, that are allowable deductions in calculating net income for tax purposes. This quantity c is simply the cost that owners of capital should charge themselves to account for the impact of tax variables, as well as rates of interest and depreciation, to insure that they are maximizing profits.

The relationship between the user cost of capital and the pace of capital formation depends, most significantly, on the form of the production function, the relationship that describes the transformation of factors of production into output. Under a rather general type of production function (a "Cobb-Douglas" production function), the desired, or optimum, amount of capital stock at any time can be represented as:

$$K^* = \alpha \ \frac{p \, Q}{c}$$

where K^* is the desired capital stock, α the elasticity of output with respect to capital (as specified in the production function), p the price of output, and Q the quantity of output, A gap between the actual level of capital stock and the desired level at a given time will initiate investment decisions designed to close that gap, and those decisions will determine the pace of capital formation. Thus, other things being equal, an increase in the cost of capital (c) will result in a reduction in the desired level of capital stock (K^*) and a consequent diminution in the rate of capital formation that would have otherwise prevailed.

The Data. The determination of income tax rates was straightforward, but there are available no direct measures of rates of property taxation; no public or private agency developed data describing the property taxes paid by various classes of manufacturers between 1911 and 1929. (The pertinent census reports of *Wealth, Debt, and Taxation* do not go beyond the geographical distribution of property taxes to measure the industrial structure of tax contributions.) Therefore, it was necessary to rely mainly on the census of manufactures and the *Statistics of Income* published annually by the Department of the Treasury since 1917 for property tax data.

The development of property tax rates for each state-industry group required ratios between all property taxes paid and fixed assets. Initially, property taxes paid by industrial groups and by states were estimated for the bench-mark years of 1909, 1919, and 1929. A direct measure of all taxes paid by industry and state is available from the Census of Manufactures for 1909 and 1919. (The industry categories used were those of the 1929 census adjusted to correspond with the categories of the *Statistics of Income*.[3])

The census data includes, however, not only property taxes paid for the years in question but, most importantly, federal excises, federal income taxes, and often state taxes, including the Wisconsin income tax. The most difficult estimate was of federal income taxes paid. Estimation posed no problem for 1909 because there were no income tax collections during that first year in which corporations incurred income tax obligations. For 1919, the best estimate for federal income taxes collected would be federal income taxes assessed on income earned in 1919. However, a disaggregation of such assessments by state and industry exists only for 1918. But it is reasonable to take the ratio of corporate income tax assessments on 1917 income to those on 1918 income within each industry group and then apply that ratio to the appropriate industry-state categories. In addition, the estimates of federal income taxes from the *Statistics of Income* required an upward adjustment to compensate for the limitation of the assessments to the corporate sector. To do this, the ratio of the value of product in the corporate sector (as determined from the *Statistics of Income*) to that for all industry (taken from the *Census of Manufactures*) was calculated for 1919 and applied to each industry-state group. Another difficulty arose from the allocation of corporate data by the Department of the Treasury to the states in terms of the "principal place of business or the principal office or agency."[4] It is impossible to estimate reliably the necessary redistribution of taxes from states to which they were allocated by the Treasury in a way that would provide conformity with the census distribution; virtually no satisfactory points of comparison exist within the data on the state distribution of firms provided by the census and by income tax data. To avoid introducing greater uncertainty, only the most clearly necessary change was made, that of adjusting the tax attributed to Illinois under the Treasury form of accounting. Otherwise, the importance of Chicago as a home office for corporations would result in an overstatement of federal income taxes paid in Illinois. To counteract this likely overstatement, we invoked the ratio of the relative size of value of product to the relative size of Illinois's share of gross income in 1919 to reduce the amount of federal income for each industry group.[5]

Next, internal revenue taxes were deducted from the "food and related products" category and the "all industry" totals.

The only adjustment made for state-levied, nonproperty taxes was the elimination of Wisconsin income taxes from each of the industry categories for Wisconsin and the total for the Great Lakes states. (Only Wisconsin of the Great Lakes states employed an income tax during this period.) As with the federal income tax, the best estimates of taxes collected in 1919 are lodged in assessments made on 1917 income. (The highly favorable collection experience under the Wisconsin income tax as well as the general one-year lag between assessment and collection, substantiate this assumption.[6]) But only the total assessment for taxes on 1917 income is available. However, the Tax Commission reported the industrial distribution of income taxes for 1919, so this distribution was applied to income taxes assessed on 1917 income. Furthermore, we ignored property tax offsets, focusing only on the income tax liability incurred and not on the manner of final payment; there is no way of knowing the proportion of income tax obligations met through the presentation of personal property tax receipts to local treasurers by industrial groups.[7] The assumption that the taxes remaining after the preceding corrections constitute property taxes produces, no doubt, something of an overstatement. This procedure does include certain miscellaneous corporation taxes levied by Illinois, Ohio, and Michigan in the property tax totals. Almost all of these taxes, however, were capital stock taxes and had an effect upon capital costs similar to that of general property taxes. Further, their estimation would have introduced greater uncertainty into the results.

The procedure for estimating property tax paid in 1929 was simpler but less reliable than that used for 1909 and 1919. The *Census of Manufactures* for 1929 did not report taxes paid by industry, so it was necessary to fall back on the estimates of the *Statistics of Income*. This source, however, provides the state and local taxes deducted from gross income only for corporations and only by national industry groups. First, we adjusted these measures upward to apply to both the noncorporate and corporate sectors. (Again, we subtracted Wisconsin income taxes. For 1929, it was possible to utilize the industrial distribution computed for 1929 assessments. Wisconsin accelerated the collection procedure with the result that assessments made in 1929 provide the best estimate for taxes collected in 1929 by industrial group.) Second, it was necessary to distribute the industry group taxes by state. We could have applied the distribution realized in 1919, but we would have either predetermined the results or ignored differential rates of growth of capital formation. The only reasonable alternative was to apply the state distribution of all state and local taxes realized in 1932 to the industry data for 1929, which assumes that the taxation of industry was an equally important source of property tax revenues in all of the states, ignores industry variations, and assumes that the distribution of property taxes among the states remained the same between 1929 and 1932. The uncertainty of this assumption necessitates a heavier reliance on the results for 1909 and 1919.

For the estimates of the value of fixed assets, the procedures used for 1909 and 1919 also yielded results more reliable than those for 1929. For the two earlier years state and industry distributions were developed from the census tabulation of capital investment (book values), again using the 1929 census industry categories, modified for consistency with the *Statistics of Income* categories.[8] The only major adjustment made was the translation of capital investment into fixed assets. The census definition of capital investment includes both fixed capital, such as land, equipment, and structures, and working capital, including inventories of material and product, bills receivable, and cash. The National Bureau of Economic Research estimates of fixed and total assets for 1904 and 1929 by industry group provided the ratios for reducing the census total-asset data.[9]

For 1929, the *Statistics of Income* offers a distribution of corporate invested capital. The first procedure was to adjust the capital data to estimate the comparable data for all industry, rather than just corporations. The *Statistics of Income* definition of invested capital was the par value of common and preferred stock as well as surplus and, of course, does not necessarily correspond to the value of fixed assets. We have the National Bureau of Economic Research estimates of the ratio between fixed and total assets, but no equally reliable estimate of the ratio of net worth to total assets. In the NBER study the authors estimated this ratio for 1919, and there is evidence of considerable stability for the net worth ratio between 1903 and 1939.[10] With these two ratios the data for invested capital was converted into estimates of fixed assets. The second procedure was to distribute fixed assets by industry among states. This involved simply the computation of total horsepower for the industry-state groups from the *Census of Manufactures for 1929* and the distribution of fixed capital within each industry group among the states in the same proportions as horsepower.

In contrast to the calculation of property tax rates, the estimation of three other components of capital costs was very straightforward. The rate of interest on municipal high-grade bonds served as the long-term interest rate, as we had it in a continuous series from 1909.[11] We calculated rates of depreciation by industry with the use of Solomon Fabricant's estimates of business depreciation charges.[12] Finally, we took the capital goods price index as the weighted average of indices for producers durables and construction materials. (Levels in 1913 were equal to 1.00.) Derivation of the weights came from relative levels of new investment in producers durables and non-residential, non-farm construction.[13] Further, we assumed that capital gains and losses were unenduring and had no impact on the demand for capital in the long run. Adopting this assumption simplifies computation and avoids introducing more uncertainty into our final estimates through an estimate of the rate of change in capital goods prices.[14]

The modifications of Wisconsin capital costs in recognition of the income tax were quite simple.[15] For one thing, property taxes on Wisconsin property were completely deductible in calculating net taxable income, so that the income tax did not increase capital costs by taxing property tax costs.

In addition, we assumed that Wisconsin corporations made full deductions for depreciation in calculating taxable income. This was the explicit intention of the Wisconsin law. The income tax law provided for the deduction of a "reasonable allowance for depreciation by use, wear and tear of property from which the income is derived."[16] A great deal of discussion and friction between the corporations and the Commission arose over what constituted a "reasonable" depreciation allowance, each side contending that it alone was in the best position to judge. Most frequently, contests occurred when corporations claimed more than the maximum rates published by the Tax Commission. Judging from the group of large corporations, the Tax Commission allowed manufacturers to take the maximum rate in most cases. The level of these rates suggests that the average depreciation rate allowed may have been reasonably close to Fabricant's estimates. The average annual rate of depreciation, according to our estimates, was slightly

more than 5% in 1919 and rose to almost 7% by 1929. Under
the maximum rates laid down in 1917, the Tax Commission
allowed 5% for frame factories, 3% for brick and masonry
factories (only 2½% for paper and pulp mills, however), and
1¼% for fireproof factories. The rates for machinery were
higher, being between 3% and 10%, while the rate for dies
was 20%, for patterns 25%, small tools 25%, and drawings
30%.[17] In 1919, the Commission specified the maximum rates
more clearly, but there was no significant alteration in their
levels.[18] These maximum rates persisted, virtually intact,
throughout the period.[19] Thus the guidelines the Tax Commission laid down seem to have been adequate to permit a
deduction of depreciation by firms doing Wisconsin business
quite in line with that taken by corporations in general. If
anything, given the low rate allowable on structure, the assumption of the complete deductibility of depreciation understates the impact of the Wisconsin income tax on capital costs
and thus lends even more conservatism to the test.

In contrast with the handling of property taxes and depreciation, we assumed that interest payments on debt financing were taxed at the full rate of 6%. Now it is true that after
1913 corporations could deduct a limited amount of interest
payments, in addition to depreciation and property taxes, in
calculating the income subject to taxation, and after 1917
they could deduct all interest payments incurred as a "cost"
to Wisconsin business. The income tax became a kind of tax
on the return on equity. But the framers of the tax were
interested in emulating the British system of using the income
taxation of corporations as a means of "collection at the
source." For this purpose, the Commission required corporations to submit complete lists of those receiving interest payments and the amounts they received. Wisconsin then taxed
the interest income of the recipients who resided in Wisconsin
at the individual income tax rates.

No way exists to determine the effective rate that resident
interest recipients paid on this income. But the law applied
the maximum rate of 6% at an early point: at income levels

in excess of $12,000. Assuming that the important sources of debt capital were Wisconsin residents with sufficiently large incomes, we took the effective rate of income taxation to be the maximum rate of 6%.[20] The assumption, in effect, means that the Wisconsin income tax bore as hard on the holders of debt capital as on the owners of equity.

If the income tax had borne more heavily on holders of equity and there had been complete flexibility with regard to debt and equity financing, we would expect a shift from equity to debt financing between 1911 and 1929. But a survey of large corporations that were incorporated in Wisconsin or had their principal place of manufacture in Wisconsin yields no such result.[21] The share of additions to debt and equity capital accounted for by debt fluctuates considerably but does not increase significantly until the late 1920's.[22] (See Table A-1.) Meanwhile, new bond issues increased in proportion to all new security issues for all manufacturing and mining corporations in the United States as a whole, through the early 1920's, and were consistently more important in the United States than in Wisconsin. (See Table A-1.) If manufacturers were unwilling to engage in debt financing, for fear of losing control of their companies, this only reinforces the assumption of the taxation of interest payments under full income tax rates, because the corporations excluded the alternative of less expensive capital.[23]

(Table A–1 on following page)

Table A–1.
New Bond Issues as a Share of All New Security Issues

Year	Debt share for large Wisconsin manufacturing corporations	Period	Debt share for large Wisconsin manufacturing corporations*	Debt share for all U.S. manufacturing and mining corporations**
1912	.1207	1911-14	.089	.218
13	.0654	1914-19	.020	.160
14	0	1919-21	.122	.344
15	.9656	1921-24	.067	.424
16	0	1924-27	.329	.348
17	.0322			
18	.0014			
19	.0046			
20	.0076			
21	.5908			
22	.1265			
23	.0028			
24	.0040			
25	0			
26	0			
27	.7064			
28	0			
29	.5349			
Average	.1902			

*1911 not available.
**SOURCE: Daniel Creamer et al., Capital in Manufacturing and Mining, p. 162.

A NOTE ON SOURCES

The most interesting sources used in this study, those that might be most profitably exploited in future research enterprise, were of an archival nature. The single most useful body of such archival material was the collection of Wisconsin corporate income tax returns. Back files of all currently active corporations are complete and are in the possession of the Wisconsin Department of Taxation. The back returns of corporations placed on an inactive basis within the last five years are also complete and on file with the Department of Taxation. All other extant discarded returns are in the custody of the State Archivist and are housed in the State Archives in the State Historical Society of Wisconsin. Permission of the Commissioner of Taxation is necessary to examine any of the returns or the corporate income tax rolls, which are in the possession of the Research Division of the Department of Taxation. Section 71.11 (44) of the *Wisconsin Statutes* makes information obtained from income tax returns confidential and prohibits publication of statistics that single out a particular taxpayer and the information taken from his return.

In addition to the extensive accumulation of discarded income tax returns, the Wisconsin State Archives also contains smaller collections relevant to the work of the Tax Commission. Most important are the papers of field auditor A. F. North, the Field Auditors Convention Papers, and the Miscellaneous Working Papers of the Tax Commission.

The delightfully abundant files of the Wisconsin Legislative Reference Library also contain much useful source material in the form of typescripts of legislative committee hearings, bound collections of bills introduced into the legislature, and staff research reports and memoranda. The collections of the State Historical Society of Wisconsin, particularly the massive papers of Charles McCarthy and Edwin E. Witte, supplement these rich archival holdings with similar material. For a full listing of such sources, see W. Elliot Brownlee, "Progressivism and Economic Growth: The Wisconsin Income Tax 1911–1929," Ph.D. dissertation, University of Wisconsin, 1969, pp. 331–335.

Apart from the Thomas Sewell Adams Papers at the Yale University Library and the Edwin R. A. Seligman Papers at the Butler Library, Columbia University, the personal papers used are found in the Manuscripts Library of the State Historical Society of Wisconsin. Of these, the most valuable were the papers of experts and progressives intimately involved in the framing and administration of Wisconsin's tax laws. These included, in addition to the Thomas S. Adams Papers, the papers of Herman L. Ekern, Nils P. Haugen, Charles McCarthy, Charles D. Rosa, and Edwin E. Witte. Less valuable were those of William J. Anderson, John R. Commons, and Richard T. Ely. The papers of John J. Blaine and Robert M. La Follette, Sr., were of service, but unfortunately the papers of Francis E. McGovern contain little of substance.

The papers of businessmen and conservatives were thinner and more disappointing, but nonetheless essential. Most interesting were those of Albert D. Bolens, Harry W. Bolens, William J. Campbell, and Emanuel L. Philipp. Less important to tax politics and policies were the papers of Stephen Bolles, Fred H. Clausen, Halbert L. Hoard, John Strange, and John M. Whitehead.

As is apparent from the citations, the study has involved extended utilization of published government documents, newspapers, periodicals, contemporary articles and books (particularly those by experts), and secondary sources, especially the literature of progressivism and the vast body of analysis of taxation and economic development.

NOTES

Introduction

1. The classic statement of this line of interpretation is Charles A. and Mary R. Beard, *The Rise of American Civilization,* Vol. II (New York, 1927), pp. 538–608. For the argument that Midwestern progressivism was a direct extrapolation of the class-oriented interests of the Populist movement, see Russel B. Nye, *Midwestern Progressive Politics: A Historical Study of Its Origins and Development, 1870–1950* (New York, 1951).

2. The initial reference is to the "status revolution" interpretation of Richard Hofstadter, *The Age of Reform* (New York, 1955), and George E. Mowry, *The California Progressives* (Chicago, 1963). The "interest-group" interpretation is found in summary in the pathbreaking analysis of Samuel P. Hays, *The Response to Industrialism, 1885–1914* (Chicago, 1957), and Robert H. Wiebe, *The Search for Order, 1877–1920* (New York, 1967), especially pp. 165–223.

3. See, especially, Gabriel Kolko, *The Triumph of Conservatism* (Chicago, 1967), and James Weinstein, *The Corporate Ideal in the Liberal State* (Boston, 1968).

4. See Albert Fishlow, "Levels of Nineteenth-Century American Investment in Education," *Journal of Economic History,* XXVI (December, 1966), pp. 418–436, and Lance E. Davis and John Legler, "The Government in the American Economy, 1815–1902: A Quantitative Study," *Journal of Economic History,* XXVI (December, 1966), pp. 513–552.

5. For a skeptical view of the contribution of government to U.S. economic growth, see Douglass C. North, *Growth and Welfare in the American Past* (Englewood Cliffs, 1965), pp. 9, 98–107, and 172–174. Entirely consistent with North's view is a theory of the rise of capitalism that stresses the importance of institutional changes designed to provide an escape from "the Malthusian trap." See North and Robert P. Thomas, "An Economic Theory of the Growth of the Western World," *The Economic Review,* XXVI (April, 1970), pp. 1–17; and North and Thomas, *The Rise of the Western World, A New Economic His-*

tory (Cambridge, England, 1973). Another recent attempt to develop a coherent theory of the development of economic institutions, including the relative role of public and private sectors, involves no general assessment of the impact of "arrangemental innovation" on American economic growth. Davis and North, "Institutional Change and American Growth: A First Step Towards a Theory of Institutional Innovation," *Journal of Economic History,* XXX (March, 1970), pp. 131–149 and *Institutional Change and American Economic Growth* (Cambridge, England 1971).

6. For a cogent rendering of this point, with regard to railroad regulation, see Robert W. Harbeson, "Railroads and Regulation, 1877–1916: Conspiracy or Public Interests?" *The Journal of Economic History,* XXVII (June, 1967), pp. 230–242.

7. See George Mowry, *The Era of Theodore Roosevelt* (New York, 1962), p. 263, and Samuel P. Hays, *The Response to Industrialism,* p. 137. Also, C. K. Yearly has recently stressed the efforts of Northern income-tax states to finance growing urban-industrial services in a more dependable fashion. Yearly, *The Money Machines* (Albany, 1970), pp. 225–250.

8. Oscar and Mary Handlin, *The Dimensions of American Liberty* (New York, 1966), pp. 83 and 178; Edwin R. A. Seligman, *The Income Tax* (New York, 1914), pp. 631–642.

9. Shigeto Tsuru, "The Economic Significance of Cities," in Oscar Handlin and John Burchard (eds.), *The Historian and the City* (Cambridge, 1963), pp. 44–55. (One can treat Tsuru's interpretation as applying in a broader sense to industrial society and not just cities.)

10. This also may be what Richard H. Wiebe means when he writes that progressive urban reformers "modernized" tax assessment to redress favoritism to "large corporations." But Wiebe does not define "modernization" in the context of tax reform, and he neglects to explain what he means by asserting that western and southern state-level progressives "rationalized tax structures." Wiebe, *The Search for Order,* pp. 168 and 180.

11. Harold U. Faulkner, in *The Decline of Laissez-Faire* (New York, 1931), argues strongly for the importance of a search for "social justice" in bringing about the federal income tax, although he does admit the possibility of a need for new sources of revenue. See p. 122. George Mowry also tends to see both objectives. See Mowry, *The Era of Theodore Roosevelt,* p. 263. Sidney Ratner, in his comprehensive *American Taxation, Its History as a Social Force in Democracy* (New York, 1942), takes the strongest view, asserting that the income tax is "regarded as preeminently fit for achieving and preserving the economic objectives of a democracy." In his view, the history of taxation in the

United States has been a struggle between "the thrust for social justice and counter-thrust for private gain." See Ratner, pp. 14 and 16. Or, consult Ratner, *Taxation and Democracy in America* (New York, 1967), pp. 14 and 16.

12. James Willard Hurst, *Law and the Conditions of Freedom in Nineteenth-Century United States* (Madison, 1964), pp. 83–84. Also C. K. Yearly finds that the federal and Southern state income taxes were designed to redistribute income toward rural folk by shifting the costs of government. See Yearly, *The Money Machines,* pp. 225–250.

13. For the relationship between Wisconsin's income tax and the adoption of income taxation elsewhere, see Chapter 3.

Numerous studies stress the significance of Wisconsin's legislation on the development of federal initiatives in social and economic legislation, including the income tax of 1913. See, for example, Joseph Dorfman, *The Economic Mind in American Civilization,* IV (New York, 1959), p. 215; Harold U. Faulkner, *The Quest for Social Justice,* 1898–1914 (New York, 1931), p. 124; Eric F. Goldman, *Rendezvous with Destiny* (New York, 1952), p. 132; Robert S. Maxwell, *La Follette and the Rise of the Progressives in Wisconsin* (Madison, 1956), pp. 199–200; Mowry, *The Era of Theodore Roosevelt,* p. 73; Nye, *Midwestern Progressive Politics,* p. 209.

14. See Nye, *Midwestern Progressive Politics,* pp. 3–32, Jorgen Weibull, "The Wisconsin Progressives, 1900–1914," *Mid-America,* XLVII (July, 1965), pp. 191–225, and Michael P. Rogin, *The Intellectuals and McCarthy: The Radical Spectre* (Cambridge, 1967), pp. 59–72.

15. In this sense, Wisconsin progressivism would be a response not so much to urbanization as to industrialization—of agriculture no less than of manufacturing. See Eric E. Lampard, *The Rise of the Dairy Industry in Wisconsin, A Study in Agricultural Change, 1820–1920* (Madison, 1963), pp. 333–351. A study that finds a clearly marked shift of governmental aid to agricultural enterprise in Wisconsin is Lewis R. Mills, *Government Fiscal Aid to Private Enterprise in Wisconsin* (unpublished S.J.D. thesis, University of Wisconsin, 1955), pp. 24 ff. and 185 ff.

16. Only recently has a historian of the Wisconsin progressive movement suggested that large corporations were able to benefit in a direct way from progressive regulatory legislation. See Stanley Caine, *The Myth of a Progressive Reform: Railroad Regulation in Wisconsin, 1903–1910* (Madison, 1970), and "Why Railroads Supported Regulation: The Case of Wisconsin, 1905–1910," *Business History Review,* XLIV (Summer, 1970), pp. 175–189.

17. David P. Thelen, *The New Citizenship: Origins of Pro-*

gressivism in Wisconsin (Columbia, Missouri, 1972). See also Albert O. Barton, *La Follette's Winning of Wisconsin* (Des Moines, 1924). Other interpretations that emphasize the diversity of interests composing the Wisconsin reform coalition but that attribute a lesser role to urban forces and underscore the personal contribution of Robert La Follette include Kenneth Acrea, "The Wisconsin Reform Coalition, 1892 to 1900: La Follette's Rise to Power," *Wisconsin Magazine of History,* 52 (Winter, 1968–69), pp. 132–157, and Herbert Margulies, *The Decline of the Progressive Movement, 1890–1920* (Madison, 1968), and Maxwell, *La Follette and The Rise of the Progressives.*

18. No historian of Wisconsin progressivism has made a clearly defined assessment of the substance of the state's income-tax movement. The best treatment of the problem is the brief one by Robert D. Maxwell, who credits the reforms fostered by the Tax Commission—including the income tax—as necessary to the rest of the progressive programs. However, he asserts that the adoption of the income tax and other tax reforms meant a victory for the "ability to pay" principle and a shift of "the bulk of the tax burden from general and personal property to corporate wealth and income," without relating this objective to that of seeking to increase the revenue productivity of the tax system. Maxwell, *La Follette and the Rise of the Progressives,* pp. 102–104.

19. The prevailing view among historians is that the Wisconsin tax had no impact on economic growth in Wisconsin, but they have relied heavily on the defense of the Wisconsin income tax offered in 1930 by Harold M. Groves and George Leffler. See Roy G. Blakey, *The State Income Tax* (Minneapolis, 1932), pp. 51–54; Leffler and Groves, *Wisconsin Industry and the Wisconsin Tax System* (Madison, 1930); and Maxwell, *La Follette and the Rise of the Progressives,* pp. 102–103.

Chapter 1

1. For examples of the best of such studies, see Wilbur R. Thompson and John M. Mattilla, *An Econometric Model of Postwar State Industrial Development* (Detroit, 1959), and Clark C. Bloom, *State and Local Tax Differentials and the Location of Manufacturing* (Iowa City, 1955).

2. For examples of hypothetical studies, see Joe S. Floyd, *Effects of Taxation on Industrial Location* (Chapel Hill, 1952), and James W. Wightman, *The Impact of State and Local Fiscal Policies on Redevelopment Areas in the Northeast, Research Report to the Federal Reserve Bank of Boston,* No. 40 (March, 1968).

Studies that give weight to taxes as a locational factor include

Edgar H. Aureswald, "The Importance of Taxes to Wisconsin Metal Manufacturing Corporations" (unpublished M.A. thesis, University of Wisconsin, 1929); Melvin L. Greenhut, *Plant Location in Theory and Practice* (Chapel Hill, 1955); Wolfgang Stolper, "Economic Development, Taxation, and Industrial Location in Michigan," *Michigan Tax Study, Staff Papers* (Lansing, 1958).

A study that compares relative tax cost differentials is William V. Williams, "A Measure of the Impact of State and Local Taxes on Industry Location," *Journal of Regional Science,* 7 (Summer, 1967), pp. 40–59.

For a more complete survey of the interest in the growth impact of state and local taxes, see John F. Due, "Studies of State-Local Tax Influences on Location of Industry," *National Tax Journal,* XIV (June, 1961), pp. 163–173. Most of the current procedures that relate taxes of states and localities to growth are simply variations on those developed to evaluate Wisconsin's tax experiments between 1911 and 1929. With the intensification of scholarly interest in economic growth, beginning with Colin Clark's *The Conditions of Economic Progress* (London, 1940), economists placed earlier procedures for assessing the growth impact of taxation into a more sophisticated theoretical framework.

3. A finding that capital was redistributed within the Great Lakes region in a sub-optimal pattern as a result of one state's tax system does not necessarily mean that there was any further reallocation beyond the region. In fact, the assumption of our study is that the impact of Wisconsin's tax system was limited to the Great Lakes states or, in other words, that the economy-wide impact was identical to the regional impact. To the extent that this was not the case, we understate the effects of Wisconsin taxes.

4. For a discussion of industrial and income changes in the Great Lakes states, see Harvey S. Perloff *et al., Regions, Resources and Economic Growth* (Baltimore, 1964), pp. 174–175, 184–190, 266–267, and 274–283.

5. Such a view of the impact on capital flows of the incidence of "partial" income taxes, which would include those with high personal exemptions, those with progressive rates, those that apply differentially to various industries, and those employed by a political subdivision of a national economy, is common in the literature of public finance. For example, see Carl S. Shoup, *Public Finance* (Chicago, 1969), pp. 338–339, and Richard A. Musgrave, *The Theory of Public Finance* (New York, 1959), p. 312.

6. For an explication and application of this "neo-classical" theory, see Dale W. Jorgenson, "Anticipations and Investment Behavior," in James S. Duesenberry (ed.), *The Brookings Quar-*

terly Econometric Model of the United States (Chicago, 1965), pp. 35–94; Jorgenson and Calvin D. Siebert, "A Comparison of Alternative Theories of Corporate Investment," *American Economic Review,* LVIII (Sept., 1968), pp. 681–712; Jorgenson and J. A. Stephenson, "Investment Behavior in U.S. Manufacturing, 1947–1960," *Econometrica,* 35 (April, 1967), pp. 167–220. Furthermore, it is arguable that other, more complex, formulations of investment behavior are consistent with and subsumed under the rubric of "profit maximization." For a description and assessment of the varying concepts of profits, see Howard J. Sherman, *Profits in the United States* (Ithaca, N.Y., 1968).

7. The assumption of perfect competition is unrealistic to some degree, but that degree is uncertain. Because of the poor state of knowledge of competition and market power during the period, it is profitable to make an assumption that permits the application of a coherent and useful body of theory to the problem. Further, an assumption of perfect competition very probably is closer to the truth than an assumption of monopolistic competition. According to one reliable estimate, "monopolistic industries" accounted for only 32% of manufacturing income in 1899 and an even smaller share, 28%, in 1937. G. Warren Nutter and Henry A. Einhorn, *Enterprise Monopoly in the United States: 1899–1958* (New York and London, 1969), p. 90. Another study finds that in 1909, 1919, and 1929, oligopolistic industries accounted only for between 16% and 21% of the value of the American manufacturing product. P. Glenn Porter and Harold C. Livesay, "Oligopolists in American Manufacturing and Their Products, 1909–1963," *Business History Review,* XLIII (Autumn 1969), pp. 282–298. Moreover, the largest corporations in Wisconsin were, at best, medium-sized by national standards and consequently lacked substantial power in the markets for their products and hence the capacity to hold up prices. Finally, it is arguable that competition in the fastest-growing industries was increasing rapidly during the 1920's. The wave of merger activity in the second half of the decade can be viewed in part as a response to this competition. This is consistent with the view of Ralph L. Nelson that this wave was "to some degree" a reflection of "the emergence of new leading industries" and constituted an attempt "to restore the industrial concentration achieved by the first merger wave." Ralph L. Nelson, *Merger Movements in American Industry, 1895–1956* (Princeton, 1959), pp. 5, 121–22, and 166.

8. For an elaboration of the definition of capital costs, taking account of local and state tax variables, see W. Elliot Brownlee, Jr., "Income Taxation and Capital Formation in Wisconsin, 1911–1929," *Explorations in Economic History,* 8 (Fall, 1970), pp. 88–90, and W. Douglas Morgan and Brownlee, "The Impact

of State and Local Taxation on Industrial Location: A New Measure," *Quarterly Review of Economics and Business,* forthcoming in 1974. The basic model was used initially to study the impact of federal income taxes. See Robert M. Coen, "Effects of Tax Policy on Investment in Manufacturing," *American Economic Review, Papers and Proceedings,* LVIII (May, 1968), pp. 200–211, and Robert E. Hall and Dale W. Jorgenson, "Tax Policy and Investment Behavior," *American Economic Review,* LVII (June, 1967), pp. 391–414. See also the Appendix.

9. For a consideration of departures from profit-maximizing behavior, the implications of such behavior for understanding reactions to income taxation, and a test of the impact of Wisconsin's income tax on capital formation, given assumptions of investment behavior divergent from those accepted as superior and applied here, see W. Elliot Brownlee, "Income Taxation and Capital Formation in Wisconsin, 1911–1929," pp. 80–88.

10. A persistent, unresolved intellectual dilemma for the "progressive" tax experts was their denial of both detrimental growth effects of Wisconsin taxation and short-run shifting of the income tax.

11. George L. Leffler and Harold M. Groves, *Wisconsin Industry and the Wisconsin Tax System* (Madison, 1930), pp. 47 and 53. A policy Wisconsin might have adopted as an attractive alternative to high income taxation or higher property taxation was an increase in state indebtedness. This would have distributed the costs of social overhead investment more equitably between present and future generations, reduced the increase in capital costs to manufacturers resulting from the income tax, made Wisconsin investment opportunities more attractive in comparison with those in neighboring states, and avoided any diminution in the level and quality of public services.

The political desirability of taxing corporate incomes evidently far outweighed the attractiveness of such an increase in indebtedness. During our period, there was no significant discussion of a repeal of Wisconsin's prohibition on state debt as a way of relieving the tax burden.

12. See Chapter Four for a discussion of the content of the agricultural service-state.

13. See the Appendix.

14. For a recent suggestion of this and similar difficulties in measuring investment behavior, see Robert Eisner, "Investment and the Frustrations of Econometricians," *The American Economic Review, Papers and Proceedings,* LIX (May, 1969), pp. 50–64.

15. As a result of the necessary limitations of the estimating

procedure for 1929, the capital-costs data is somewhat less reliable for that year than for 1909 and 1919. See the Appendix.

16. The 1925 legislature removed a provision of the original act that had allowed taxpayers to apply any personal property tax paid to their income tax obligations; the change increased the total tax bills of manufacturers. At the same time, the formula by which the income tax revenues were distributed was altered to increase the share retained by the state from 10% to 40%. The resultant loss in revenues to urban-industrial counties and localities was considerably greater than any gains realized from repeal of the offset; the consequence was increased financial pressure on these counties and localities and a correspondingly heightened incentive to tax manufacturing property. Harley Lutz, "Memorandum on the Revision of the Wisconsin Income Tax," December 15, 1924, in Herman L. Ekern Papers, State Historical Society of Wisconsin (SHSW).

17. Property taxation outweighted the contribution of income taxation to capital costs, at least in 1919. The state income tax thus failed to reduce the relative rate of industrial property taxation, as many progressives had claimed it would. Moreover, although county and local governments set most of the industrial property tax burden, they had to operate within a framework of state law that strongly favored nonmanufacturing corporations in local property taxation. See Chapter 3.

18. These surtaxes yielded revenues that the state monopolized for special purposes. See Chaper 4.

19. The possibility that "out-migration" of firms contributed to this reallocation is small, given the high levels of capital commitment and the often prohibitive moving costs within the major industries. Almost none of the notorious cases widely discussed during the 1920's involved an outright physical transfer of plant facilities. The "pro-business" series of articles on the effect of taxes on industry development by Robert A. Kennedy that appeared in the *Green Bay Press-Gazette* in 1925 (August 31-September 17) implicitly substantiated this conclusion. The nature of the political issue tended to direct interest toward the most easily visualized phenomenon: the actual physical removal of a firm's plant.

20. This is further supported by the fact that the annual rate of growth of real capital in the metals industries in the United States was significantly higher during the period from 1914 to 1919 than in the following ten years. In the critical metal industries, capital increased at the annual rates of 3.6% during 1909–14 and 7.1% during 1914–19, as contrasted with the low rate of 1.2% between 1919 and 1929. Daniel Creamer *et al.*, *Capital in Manufacturing and Mining, Its Formation and Financing* (Princeton, 1960), p. 25.

21. By the early twentieth century, capital users had made the transition from "immobile" to "mobile" capital. Savers had become willing to invest in areas removed from their own first-hand experience, and capital markets and financial intermediaries (such as investment bankers, commercial bankers, and insurance companies) had matured to facilitate capital mobility. See Lance E. Davis, "Capital Immobilities and Finance Capitalism: A Study of Economic Evolution in the United States, 1820–1920," *Explorations in Entrepreneurial History, Second Series,* I (Fall, 1963), pp. 88–105, and Davis, "The Investment Market, 1870–1914; The Evolution of a National Market," *The Journal of Economic History,* XXV (Sept., 1965), pp. 355–99.

22. For the theoretical relationship between capital costs, desired levels of capital stock, and investment, see references in note 8 and the Appendix.

23. An introduction to the analysis of federal income taxation, in addition to the other sources cited, is Joseph A. Pechman, *Federal Tax Policy* (Washington, D.C., 1966). See also Musgrave, *The Theory of Public Finance,* pp. 160–183, 232–287, and 312–346; Shoup, *Public Finance,* pp. 291–343; and National Bureau of Economic Research and the Brookings Institution, *The Role of Direct and Indirect Taxes in the Federal Revenue System* (Princeton, 1964).

For a highly skeptical view of the heavy taxation of profits and incomes by a developing nation because of the risk posed to necessary capital formation, see W. Arthur Lewis, *The Theory of Economic Growth* (Homewood, Ill., 1955), pp. 201–303 and 376–419. It remains to be seen how such a warning should apply to federal income taxation during the progressive era.

24. The most comprehensive analysis of the "bads" ignored in calculations of the value of goods and services is Ezra J. Mishan, *The Costs of Economic Growth* (New York, 1967). On the assessment of environmental issues during the progressive era a useful source is Roderick Nash (ed.), *The American Environment, Readings in the History of Conservation* (Reading, Mass., 1968), pp. 37–93.

25. For a discussion of these and related points, including the economic desirability of accepting some modest level of pollution, the possible solutions to the problems of pollution within the framework of the marketplace and economic growth, the likelihood of finding technological solutions to central energy and raw material shortages, the disassociation between the problems of population growth and economic growth, and the environmental benefits, both political and economic, of sustained economic growth, see W. Elliot Brownlee, *The Dynamics of Ascent:*

A History of the American Economy (New York, 1974), pp. 347–367.

26. See Chapter 4.

Chapter 2

1. For arguments as to the necessity of increased rates of saving and capital formation to the processes of industrialization and economic growth, see Alexander Gerschenkron, *Economic Backwardness in Historical Perspective, A Book of Essays* (Cambridge, 1962), and W. Arthur Lewis, *The Theory of Economic Growth* (Homewood, Ill. 1955), especially pp. 201–303. For evidence of the rapid increase in the share of national product devoted to capital formation ensuing after the Civil War, see Robert E. Gallman, "Gross National Product in the United States, 1834–1909," Conference on Income and Wealth, *Output, Employment and Productivity in the United States after 1800,* National Bureau of Economic Research, *Studies in Income and Wealth,* Vol. 30 (New York, 1966), p. 11.

Some recent studies have tended to question the earlier emphasis on the contribution of capital to modern economic growth and to emphasize instead the role played by labor. However, these studies have failed to adjust their measures of capital input for the quality of capital services, thus underestimating the contribution of that factor. Another, more recent, line of inquiry indicates that the role of capital input may explain almost one half of the increase in national product even for the period since 1929, when tangible capital (buildings and structures) presumably has played a lesser role than earlier in the growth of output. For the latter argument see Zvi Griliches and Dale W. Jorgenson, "Sources of Measured Productivity Change: Capital Input," *American Economic Review,* LVI (May, 1966), pp. 5–61, and for the former interpretation, see Edward F. Denison, *The Sources of Economic Growth in the United States and the Alternatives Before Us* (New York, 1962).

2. See Chapter One, n. 21.

3. For an excellent discussion of these locational changes, see Richard A. Easterlin, "Redistribution of Manufacturing," in Simon Kuznets *et al., Population Redistribution and Economic Growth, United States, 1870–1950, Analyses of Economic Change,* II (Philadelphia, 1960), pp. 103–122.

4. This fact casts serious doubt on an explanation that would attribute Wisconsin's relatively poor performance to a relatively small automobile industry.

5. The fact that Wisconsin's aggregate wage rate fell significantly behind that of the region as a whole does not mean that the wage rate fell within each or any category of employment.

Indeed, Wisconsin's relative wage rate could have easily increased or remained the same for every category of employment; the relative shift of employment toward lower-wage occupations was sufficient to have offset a pattern of increases. The problems of correctly disaggregating the labor supply by productivity classes precludes a systematic exploration of this problem within the scope of the present study, but a preliminary examination suggests that, in fact, relative real wage levels were either remaining constant or rising in Wisconsin. For example, in the automobile industry, while wage levels in Wisconsin were equal to the average of those prevailing in the region in 1909 ($637 per worker per year), by 1919 they were 11% higher than the $1,304 that was the average for the region. For the three largest metal-using industries in Wisconsin in 1909 and 1919—the automobile, foundry and machine shop products, and agricultural machinery and implement industries—wages were about equal to the regional average. In each year, Wisconsin's average wage per worker was less than 1% removed from the regional average. U.S. Department of Commerce, Bureau of the Census, *Thirteenth Census,* Vol. IX, *Manufactures, 1909,* (Washington, D.C., 1912), pp. 292–295, 328–331, 578–581, 984–989, and 1356–1359; *Fourteenth Census,* Vol. IX, *Manufactures, 1919* (Washington, D.C., 1923), pp. 348–359, 400–407, 698–705, and 1638–1645.

6. See ch. 1, sec. 3 and ch. 4, sec. 3.

7. Harless D. Waggoner, *The U.S. Machine Tool Industry from 1900 to 1950* (Cambridge, 1968), p. 57. The same appears to have been true for the highly dynamic aluminum cookware industry. James M. Rock, "A Growth Industry: The Wisconsin Aluminum Cookware Industry, 1893–1920," *Wisconsin Magazine of History,* 55 (Winter, 1971–72) ,pp. 97–99.

8. The pattern of relatively constant or increasing wages in Wisconsin provides evidence that Wisconsin manufacturers did not seek to maintain production levels in the face of increasing capital costs by shifting to the use of a larger input of labor. Such a course would have been economical only if Wisconsin's wage rate had fallen. (Evidence on wage movements does not, however, rule out the possibility that Wisconsin manufacturers developed and adopted a unique technology to increase total factor productivity. However, no evidence exists to indicate such a development; in all probability, such a technology would have been attractive to many manufacturers outside Wisconsin facing even a different ratio between the price of capital and the price of labor. Thus, it is reasonable to assume that if Wisconsin manufacturers had developed such a competitive advantage, they would not have been able to maintain it for a significant length of time.)

9. For a recent example of the use of illiteracy rates in the

measure of relative levels of skills, see Robert Higgs, "Race, Skills, and Earnings: American Immigrants in 1909," *Journal of Economic History,* XXXI (June, 1971), pp. 420–428.

10. See Table 2-E for the sources of the productivity data (value added per member of the labor force).

11. For a persuasive argument to this effect, see Edwin E. Witte, "Wisconsin's Industrial Progress in Recent Years," June 1926, in files of the Wisconsin Legislative Reference Library, and Witte, "Some Reasons Why Manufacturing Plants Should Locate in Wisconsin Rather than in Illinois," April 6, 1928, Edwin E. Witte Papers, SHSW. For evidence that the current situation conforms to Witte's description, see Federal Reserve Bank of Chicago, *Annual Report,* 1956 (Chicago, 1956), pp. 22–40.

12. Harold F. Williamson and Kenneth H. Myers, *Designed for Digging, The First 75 Years of Bucyrus-Erie Company* (Evanston, 1955), pp. 121–122.

13. Waggoner, *The U.S. Machine Tool Industry,* pp. 40–44, 46–51, 73–75, 83–92, 113, 119–136, and 366–368.

14. Easterlin, "Redistribution of Manufacturing," pp. 109 and 121.

15. For the relative levels of taxation, see pages 42–43.

Chapter 3

1. On the relationship between corporation taxation in general and taxation of manufacturers in particular, see pp. 56–59. For the outlines of the development of corporate taxation in the nineteenth century, see Edwin R. A. Seligman, *Essays in Taxation* (New York, 1921), especially pp. 145–220.

2. This group of industrial states was joined in their taxation of corporate incomes by Mississippi (1912), Oklahoma (1915), West Virginia (1915), Montana (1917), Missouri (1917), Delaware (1917), Virginia (1918), Alabama (1919), North Carolina (1919), and North Dakota (1919). With the exception of the modernization of South Carolina's tax and the adoption of a very rudimentary income tax in New Hampshire, no state adopted income taxation of any sort between 1919 and 1929. Roy G. Blakey, *The State Income Tax* (Minneapolis, 1932), pp. 10–71; Alzada Comstock, *State Taxation of Personal Incomes* (N.Y., 1921), pp. 17 ff.; Harley L. Lutz, "The Progress of State Income Taxation Since 1911," *American Economic Review,* X (March, 1920), pp. 66–91; Truman C. Bigham, "Fiscal Aspects of the State Income Tax Since 1918," *American Economic Review,* XIX (June, 1929), pp. 227–245.

3. The rates cited are maximum rates. See E. E. Witte,

"Summary of some Features of State Income Tax Laws as of January 1, 1923, Contrasted with the Federal Income Tax Law and the Model Personal Income Tax Law of the National Tax Association," copy in Herman Ekern papers, Box #45, State Historical Society of Wisconsin (SHSW); Beatrice Hagen and Witte, "Summary of Some Features of The Laws Relating to The Taxation of The Personal Property, Machinery and Fixtures of Manufacturers and Merchants in all States," September, 1926, typescript in files of The Wisconsin Legislative Reference Library (WLRL).

4. In California, however, the redirection of reform interest toward the communal role of manufacturers involved less interest in taxation than in Wisconsin. The history of California tax reforms remains to be placed in a comparative analytical framework, but an explanation of the contrasts with Wisconsin seems to rest in the stronger resistance of California communities to relinquishing the power of taxation to the state and, most significantly for the manufacturers, the ability of labor to buffer progressive interest in taxing industry. The Socialists played a similar role in Wisconsin, but they constituted a far more limited element in the progressive coalition. See pp. 61 and 63. For an analysis of the powerful contribution of labor to the electoral strength of California progressives, see Michael Rogin and John Shover, *Political Change in California* (Westport, Conn., 1970), Chapter Three. The basic histories of California tax development are William C. Frankhauser, *A Financial History of California* (Berkeley, 1913), and Manuel M. Stockwell, *Studies in California State Taxation, 1910–1935* (Berkeley, 1939), in which pp. 124–257 focus on business and income taxation.

5. For data on the structure of the labor force and the scale of manufacturing in selected states, see W. Elliot Brownlee, Jr., "Progressivism and Economic Growth: The Wisconsin Income Tax, 1911–1929," Ph.D. diss. U. of Wisc., 1969, pp. 29–30.

6. The role of cultural factors in shaping electoral politics in Wisconsin during the 1890's has received extensive analysis in Richard Jensen, *The Winning of the Midwest: Social and Political Conflict, 1888–1896* (Chicago, 1971); Paul Kleppner, *The Cross of Culture: A Social Analysis of Midwestern Politics, 1850–1900* (New York, 1970); and Roger E. Wyman, "Wisconsin Ethnic Groups and the Election of 1890," *Wisconsin Magazine of History*, 51 (Summer, 1968), pp. 269–293. For the shift of Wisconsin electoral cleavages to a class basis beginning in the late 1890's, see Jorgan Weibull, "The Wisconsin Progressives, 1900–1914," *Mid-America*, XLVII (July, 1965), pp. 191–225; Michael P. Rogin, *The Intellectuals and McCarthy: The Radical Specter* (Cambridge, 1967); and Roger E. Wyman, "Voting Behavior in The Progressive Era; Wisconsin as a Case Study"

(Ph.D. dissertation, Univ. of Wisconsin, 1970). Another recent study finds that "class" was the only characteristic distinguishing between the progressive and the stalwart leadership groups. Mark Lieberman, "Progressivism, Wisconsin, and the Status Revolution," *Explorations in Entrepreneurial History*, Second Series, 6 (Spring-Summer, 1969), pp. 297–308.

7. See, especially, Edwin R. A. Seligman, "Recent Reports on State and Local Taxation," *American Economic Review*, I (June, 1911), pp. 272–295, and C. K. Yearly, *The Money Machines* (Albany, 1970), pp. 167–250.

8. Such dissatisfaction had surfaced at least as early as 1867, with the report of a state Tax Commission. State of Wisconsin, *Report of the Tax Commissioners*, 1867, pp. 5–6, 9.

9. On the activities of the urban tax reformers, see David P. Thelen, *The New Citizenship* (Columbia, Missouri, 1972), pp. 203–211.

10. State of Wisconsin, Tax Commission, *Report*, 1898, p. 74, 109–110, 167–168; *Milwaukee Sentinel*, February 8, 1898.

11. Speech of Robert M. La Follette, "Dangers Threatening Representative Government," July 4, 1897, Robert M. La Follette Papers, Box #7, State Historical Society of Wisconsin (La Follette made no reference to income taxation in this speech); State of Wisconsin Tax Commission, *Report*, 1898, p. 72.

La Follette's estimate was, in fact, a considerable exaggeration. A Milwaukee member of the 1897 Tax Commission, Kossuth K. Kennan, pointed out that La Follette had compared the "equalized" value of horses with the local value for intangibles; a true comparison would have yielded a figure of the order of $1.4 million. In contrast with La Follette, Kennan was more concerned about the way underassessment of intangibles increased taxation of urban real estate and tangible personal property than about the way such underassessment raised taxes on farm property. Kossuth K. Kennan to Robert M. La Follette, September 27, 1897, La Follette Papers, State Historical Society of Wisconsin; *Milwaukee Sentinel*, February 8, 1898.

12. For evidence of the agricultural focus of support for federal income taxation, see Sidney Ratner, *American Taxation, Its History as a Social Force in Democracy* (New York, 1942), pp. 172–214, and Elmer Ellis, "Public Opinion and the Income Tax, 1860–1900," *Mississippi Valley Historical Review*, XXVII (September, 1940), pp. 225–242. For recent support for this interpretation, see C. K. Yearly, *The Money Machines*, pp. 230 ff.

13. On the consensus among experts with regard to the potential benefits to farmers from income taxation, see Yearly, *The Money Machines*, pp. 277 ff.

14. Edwin R. A. Seligman, "The Relations of State and Federal Finance," in *Proceedings of the Third International Conference on State and Local Taxation Under the Auspices of the International Tax Association,* September 21-24, 1909, pp. 213-226; Seligman, *Essays in Taxation* (New York, 1895), pp. 403-404; Seligman, *The Income Tax* (New York, 1911). For similar views, see Francis Walker, "The Taxation of Corporations in the United States," *Annals of the American Academy of Political and Social Science,* March, 1902, pp. 165-184, and Charles J. Bullock (of Harvard University) to E. R. A. Seligman, August 7, 1911, in the Thomas Sewell Adams Papers, Yale University Library.

15. Once the federal government had successfully adopted full-scale income taxation in 1913 and state income taxation gained increasing political support in Connecticut and New York, Seligman began to look favorably on limited state income taxes and participated, along with Thomas S. Adams, in the drafting of income taxes in those two states. Seligman apparently believed that the federal tax paved the way for administratively successful state income taxes and may well have seized an opportunity to advance his own consulting career and, at the same time, to advance the financial welfare of the New York real estate interests with which he was associated. However, both Seligman and Adams favored granting manufacturing corporations a protected status with the system of income taxation as a way of protecting industrial prosperity. To Seligman, the Wisconsin tax system was interesting for its advances in administrative reform rather than its treatment of corporate income. Edwin R. A. Seligman, "The New York Income Tax," *Political Science Quarterly,* XXXIV (December, 1919), pp. 521-545; Presidential Address of Edwin R. A. Seligman delivered at the Ninth Annual Conference of the National Tax Association, August 11, 1915, typescript in Edwin R. A. Seligman Papers, Butler Library, Columbia University; Seligman correspondence, 1914-16, Seligman Papers; Nils P. Haugen to Thomas S. Adams, Oct. 20, 1915, Haugen Papers, SHSW.

16. For his initial position, see Richard T. Ely, *Taxation in American States and Cities* (New York, 1888), p. 287. On his later development, see Ely, "Questions of the Day: Reforms in Taxation," *Cosmopolitan,* XXX (January, 1901); *Outlines of Economics* (New York, 1901), p. 361; and entries in the "Seminary Minutes," Richard T. Ely Papers, State Historical Society of Wisconsin, November 15, 1899, and March 13, 1900. (The 1901 *Cosmopolitan* article was actually written "four or five" years earlier. January 15, 1901, entry in the Seminary Minutes.)

17. Delos O. Kinsman, *The Income Tax in the Common-*

wealths of the United States (New York, 1903), and Kossuth K. Kennan, *Income Taxation* (Milwaukee, 1910).

18. State of Wisconsin, Tax Commission, *Report,* 1898, pp. 167–168; *1909,* pp. 17–21.

19. In fact, the discredited license fees applied by the state to certain utilities resembled a form of income taxation, while *ad valorem* taxation, the central proposal of those wishing utility tax reform, was simply a kind of property tax. For a discussion of the taxation of non-manufacturing corporations, see pp. 56–59.

20. See, once again, for emphasis on issues of taxation and regulation of corporations in the development of Wisconsin urban reform during the 1890's, David P. Thelen, *The New Citizenship,* especially pp. 203–211, and Thelen, "Social Tensions and the Origins of Progressivism," *The Journal of American History,* LVI (Sept., 1969), pp. 337–341.

21. On the relationship between the interests of manufacturers and taxation of banks and utilities, see pp. 56–59.

22. Banks fell under the heavy taxation of state and local property taxes applied to the very easily assessed cash value of their stock. Thus, the banks paid property taxes through shareholders whose shares were assessed at cash value, a matter of public record, and taxed at the rate applied to other property in their taxing district, which was usually assessed at less than cash value. Raymond V. Phelan, *The Financial History of Wisconsin* (Madison, 1908), pp. 373–413; State of Wisconsin, Tax Commission, *Report, 1898,* p. 157; *1901,* p. 71.

23. State of Wisconsin, Tax Commission, *Report, 1903,* pp. 95 ff.

24. The progressive Milwaukee *Free Press,* as well as the "stalwart" Milwaukee *Sentinel,* supported the exemption of mortgages from property taxation in 1903 and then, in 1905, opposed a return to that taxation. The leading argument was that taxing mortgages under local rates would prevent Milwaukee creditors from competing with lenders from other cities. Editorials in *Milwaukee Free Press,* May 30, June 6, and June 17, 1905; "Taxation of Mortgages," *Milwaukee Free Press,* April 27, 1905, and letter from Wade H. Richardson, *Milwaukee Free Press,* May 22, 1905. Richardson was a Milwaukee real estate dealer and spokesman for the Milwaukee Real Estate Board.

25. For assessments of the role of Haugen in the development of Wisconsin progressivism, see Robert S. Maxwell, *La Follette and the Rise of the Progressives,* pp. 87–104, and Stuart D. Brandes, "Nils P. Haugen and the Wisconsin Progressive Movement" (unpublished M.S. thesis, University of Wisconsin, 1965). For analysis of the significance of the Scandinavian voters to the progressive coalition, see Michael P. Rogin, *The Intellec-*

tuals and McCarthy, pp. 59–72, and Jorgen Weibull, "The Wisconsin Progressives," pp. 191–225. The central place of Haugen and his supporters in the Republican coalition suggest the significance of the merger of class and ethnic appeals to the Scandinavian population in the development of the progressive coalition in Wisconsin.

For data on Haugen's investments, see his account book 17 in Box #70 of the Nils P. Haugen Papers, SHSW. For a typical statement of the disadvantage institutional lenders feared they would suffer under credit exemption, see B. J. Morse to Haugen, June 11, 1903, Haugen Papers. (A close business associate and friend of Haugen, Morse was Secretary of the Mt. Morris Norwegian Fire Insurance Company.)

26. For Haugen's income tax proposal, see State of Wisconsin, Tax Commission, *Report, 1903,* pp. 260–261, Haugen, "The Exemption of Credits," speech before the Assembly Committee on the Assessment and Collection of Taxes, April 22, 1903, copy in files of the WLRL, and Haugen to B. J. Morse, March 26, 1903, Haugen Papers.

Writing to a close friend, Haugen expressed fear that the exemption of credits issue would get "in the way of the other and more vital issues," meaning railroad tax proposals. Haugen to B. J. Morse, Feb. 21, 1903, and Haugen to J. Grimm, Feb. 24, 1903, in Haugen Papers.

While Milwaukee progressives, with their real estate interests, were unenthusiastic about the prospect of income taxation, La Follette and rural progressives, including La Follette's successor, James O. Davidson, and legislator Andrew H. Dahl, kept the possibility of stiff credit taxation before them. Consequently, the Milwaukee element tended to accept income taxation as a preferable alternative to a vigorously enforced property taxation and the final income tax measure provided for the exemption of all intangibles from property taxation. See n. 24 and n. 64, this chapter. "Governor's Message, 1905," copy in files of WLRL; *Milwaukee Sentinel,* May 18, 1905; Haugen to Robert M. La Follette, January 12, 1907, in Haugen Papers.

27. State of Wisconsin, *Wisconsin Blue Book* (Madison, 1909), p. 558.

28. In making his original income tax proposal of 1903, he referred for justification to Ely's Maryland report, ignoring Ely's subsequent reversal and the criticism that Ely made of Haugen's credit exemption suggestion. In that original proposal, Haugen also misrepresented the ideas of Edwin R. A. Seligman, ignoring not only his extensive criticism of state income taxation but also his strong critique of Ely's Maryland recommendation (which appeared in the very same volume that Haugen

cited to support his own recommendation). Nils P. Haugen, "The Exemption of Credits," p. 6; Haugen, *Pioneer and Political Reminiscences* (Evansville, Wisconsin, 1920), pp. 155–156; Seminary Minutes, April 28 and May 5, 1903, Richard T. Ely Papers, SHSW; Edwin R. A. Seligman, *Essays in Taxation* (New York, 1895), pp. 403–404.

29. His only pertinent research was limited to a study of the impact of the exemption of mortgages on interest rates. Thomas S. Adams, "Mortgage Taxation in Wisconsin," *The Quarterly Journal of Economics,* XXII (Nov., 1907), pp. 1–27.

30. Haugen, "The Taxation of Credits and Money," *Papers and Proceedings of the First Annual Meeting of the Minnesota Academy of Social Sciences,* Dec. 6, 1907, pp. 138–168; *The Evening Wisconsin,* Milwaukee, March 30, 1907.

31. For example, see "The Proposed Amendment," *Milwaukee Sentinel,* Oct. 18, 1904, and "Income Tax is a Delusion," speech by Pliny Norcross in *Milwaukee Sentinel,* March 25, 1905.

32. Ratner, *American Taxation, Its History as a Social Force in Democracy,* pp. 267–69, 280–307; Robert M. La Follette, "The Propertyless Man and the Income Tax," *La Follette's Weekly Magazine,* May 15, 1909; La Follette, "Who Pays the Tax?" *La Follette's Weekly Magazine,* July 17, 1909; *Milwaukee Journal,* July 15, 1909.

33. *Wisconsin State Journal,* Madison, Feb. 19, 1909; *Milwaukee Free-Press,* March 21, 1909 and July 31, 1909.

The framers of the 1909 measures took their wording from the federal income tax of 1894. But, in distinction from the flat rate of 2% levied on all incomes over $4,000 incorporated in the federal law, the Wisconsin bill proposed a graduated tax on all incomes over $500, reaching a maximum rate of 20% on incomes, both personal and corporate, over $170,000. In further distinction, the 1909 measure made no allowance for the deduction of interest payments by corporations in calculating net income. Assembly Bill No. 831 A, Feb. 25, 1909, copy in files of WLRL.

34. *Milwaukee Free-Press,* Feb. 16, 1910.

35. See n. 17, this chapter. Kennan, *Income Taxation, Methods and Results in Various Countries,* pp. 235–236, 307–325. (The MMMA provided Kennan's book with an extremely laudatory review. *Civics and Commerce,* January, 1911.)

36. Milwaukee Merchants and Manufacturers Association, *Bulletin,* March and April-May, 1910, and *Milwaukee Free-Press,* April 4, 1910.

37. Perhaps the best example of such an industry was machine-tool manufacturing, including large, politically active firms

such as the Falk Corporation, The Filer and Stowell Co., Fairbanks-Morse Co., and the Gisholt Co. of Madison. On the pre-
dominance of small-scale enterprise within the machine-tool industry, with an implication of competitive market conditions,
see Harless D. Waggoner, *The U.S. Machine Tool Industry from
1900 to 1950* (Cambridge, 1968), pp. 46–51, 73–75, 119–136, and
366–368. More generally, market conditions within all the non-
electrical machinery producers, central in Wisconsin's manufacturing community, appeared highly competitive in 1909; among
machinery producers, oligopolists produced only 16% of product
value and, among fabricated metals producers, oligopolists accounted for only 2% of product value. Alfred D. Chandler, Jr.,
"The Structure of American Industry in the Twentieth Century:
A Historical Overview," *Business History Review,* XLIII (Autumn, 1969), 259.

38. *Civics and Commerce,* Milwaukee, Oct. and Nov., 1910;
Milwaukee Sentinel, Jan. 18, 1911.

39. See Alfred D. Chandler, Jr., *Strategy and Structure,
Chapters in the History of Industrial Enterprise* (Cambridge,
Mass., 1962), pp. 173–174, for the development of institutional
innovation within corporations such as the introduction of inter-
divisional billing at market prices at General Motors by Donaldson Brown. A far less commonly used technque, given the string-
ency of Wisconsin tax administration, was the resort to the use
of sales corporations within holding companies or special sales
contracts by interstate corporations to evade the Wisconsin tax.
Wisconsin almost always successfully prosecuted such corporations. One such prosecution was of Buick Motor Company,
which had limited its income from its Wisconsin branch to a
negligible amount through a contract with the General Motors
Company, despite Donaldson Brown's lauded financial controls.
Wisconsin extracted $232,000 in back taxes. See Wisconsin Tax
Commission, *Report,* 1930, pp. 195–196; "Additional Corporation Income and Taxes, together with interest on the Additional
Taxes as a result of Field Audits reported subsequent to closing
of 1925 Tax Roll and up to September 30, 1926," in Miscellaneous Working Papers of the Wisconsin Tax Commission, Wisconsin State Archives. For another significant case, see *Palm-
olive Co. v. Conway et al.,* 43 Fed (2nd), 226; and for an account
of the use of holding companies by industrial enterprises that
places greater emphasis on tax-cost considerations than does
Chandler, see James C. Bonbright and Gardiner C. Means, *The
Holding Company, Its Public Significance and Its Regulation*
(New York and London, 1932), pp. 66–89. For a discussion of
the relationship between the activities of these interstate corporations and the Wisconsin tax system, see W. Elliot Brownlee,

"Progressivism and Economic Growth: The Wisconsin Income Tax, 1911–1929," pp. 112–125.

40. William George Bruce, untitled report to the Common Council of the City of Milwaukee, Jan. 9, 1905, copy in files of WLRL; Bruce, "Local Taxation and the Businessman," Bulletin, Sept., 1906; *Milwaukee Free-Press*, Oct. 15, 1906; *Bulletin*, Nov., 1906.

41. One needs to distinguish the position of the railroads on the adoption of the *ad valorem* tax basis from their opposition to the level of taxes levied or to the application of the state-wide general property tax rate to their assessed valuation. While the railroads bitterly fought the efforts of the progressives to increase their taxes, there is evidence that they were much more concerned about the extension of the gross receipts tax than the introduction of the *ad valorem* system. For strong suggestions of this, see Emanuel L. Philipp, *Political Reform in Wisconsin* (Milwaukee, 1910), pp. 138–178. For other evidence as to the lack of railroad concern as to *ad valorem* taxation, see Stanley P. Caine, *The Myth of a Progressive Reform, Railroad Regulation in Wisconsin, 1903–1910* (Madison, 1970), p. 52. The thrust of the railroad regulation imposed by the Railroad Commission Act of 1905 was to guarantee the railroads a "reasonable" rate of return after taxes. See Edward J. Brabant, "The Valuation of Public Utilities for Taxation," *Bulletin of The National Tax Association*, VII (June, 1922), pp. 280–288.

42. The state government found the interests of the street railways congenial, because the state, like the cities, was strapped for funds during the depression of the 1890's and there was increasing desire to reduce reliance on the property tax at the state level. Greater reliance on corporate taxes at the state level offered the likelihood of reducing the competitive undervaluation of property by counties trying to reduce their share of the state's general property tax. For a discussion of the advantages to assessment procedures of a reliance on centralized taxation of corporations, see State of Wisconsin, Tax Commission, *Report,* 1898, p. 158; 1901, pp. 158–159.

43. The *ad valorem* method of taxing railroads remained fundamentally unchanged throughout the period. But, to the extent that the assessment of manufacturing and noncorporate property under the general property tax improved during the period, the relative position of the corporations taxed under the *ad valorem* system improved; the higher the general level of assessment, the lower the general tax rate and the lower the taxes extracted from the utilities, with a given revenue requirement. Thus, the interest of the progressives in increasing assessments of manufacturing property coincided with the interest of the utilities in lower taxes. Finally, the setting aside of state

property tax assessments in 1926 and 1927, facilitated by an increase in the taxation of manufacturers, reduced the tax rate applied to utilities under *ad valorem* taxation. Floyd F. Burtchett, "Development of the Fiscal System of Wisconsin, 1900–1925," unpublished Ph.D. dissertation, University of Wisconsin, 1927, Chapters 14–16; Raymond V. Phelan, *The Financial History of Wisconsin* (Madison, 1908), pp. 373–413; Wisconsin Tax Commission, "Taxes of the State of Wisconsin and its Political Subdivisions, 1901–1936," *Bulletin No. 76* (August, 1936), 1–10, 18–19. For a full description of the railroad license fee system and a critique of *ad valorem* taxation, see Guy Edward Snider, *The Taxation of The Gross Receipts of Railways in Wisconsin* (New York, 1906).

44. Copy of Bill 158-A as reported by the Special Committee on the Income Tax, files in WLRL; *Milwaukee Daily News,* November 19, 1909. (Insurance companies paid their taxes on a receipts basis, with virtually all the revenues retained by the state.)

Haugen, once again representing the interests of the banking community, was responsible for the suggestion of exempting insurance companies and banks. S. M. Marsh to Haugen, Dec. 30, 1909, in Haugen Papers.

45. Testimony of E. R. Bowler, Feb. 7, 1911. Joint Hearings on the income tax, typescript in files of the WLRL.

46. "State Income Tax Opposed," *Civics and Commerce,* Feb., 1911; Testimony of Paul D. Carpenter, Feb. 7, 1911, and Hugh Ryan, Feb. 28, 1911, Joint Hearings on the income tax, typescripts in WLRL. Part of the fear of the Milwaukee manufacturers grew out of the recent victory of the Social Democrats in city government and the possibility of larger public expenditures on municipal enterprises. They believed that the income tax, by turning 85% of the revenues over to the cities while leaving the property tax intact, would only encourage extravagance and not decrease property taxes. *Civics and Commerce,* Jan., 1911; *Milwaukee Sentinel,* Jan. 1, Jan. 4, Jan. 15, and Feb. 7, 1911. The leadership of the effort to stem increases in local property taxes was in the hands of a Committee on Taxation under Kossuth K. Kennan.

47. See n. 39, *supra.*

48. Testimony of Paul D. Carpenter, Feb., 1911, files of WLRL; Harry W. Bolens. "Memorandum on Wisconsin Income Tax Bill No. 158-A," in Harry W. Bolens Papers, SHSW.

49. *Civics and Commerce,* February, 1911; Testimony of Paul D. Carpenter, Feb., 1911, files of WLRL.

50. The Wisconsin manufacturers appear to have become convinced that adoption of federal income taxation would in no

way reduce the enthusiasm of Wisconsin progressives for their own state income tax. In 1912, the Wisconsin manufacturers did attempt, through their influence in the conservative Milwaukee organization of the Wisconsin Democratic Party, to include in the national party platform a plank recommending the enactment of federal income taxation to replace state income taxes. But when the replacement plank failed to gain convention approval, the manufacturers abandoned interest in using federal taxation to preclude Wisconsin initiatives. *Milwaukee Free Press,* June 29, 1912.

Thus, although the Wisconsin income tax movement may well substantiate Gabriel Kolko's suspicion that state-level progressives were often more radical than their federal-level counterparts, the political activities of Wisconsin manufacturers provide no support for his conclusion that businessmen successfully conspired to preclude more threatening state initiatives by promoting progressive federal legislation. Kolko, *The Triumph of Conservatism* (Chicago, 1967), especially pp. 5–6 and 161–163.

51. *Milwaukee Free Press,* June 15, 1911. There was no evidence that Milwaukee Socialists were eager to pass the tax in order to augment city revenues, as the manufacturers had once claimed. In fact, the Milwaukee manufacturers had ceased to make this charge by the time of the final legislative deliberations. Winfield R. Gaylord (Social Democratic senator from Milwaukee) to Charles McCarthy, June 18, 1912, Charles McCarthy Papers, SHSW; *Milwaukee Daily News,* June 29, 1911; *Milwaukee Sentinal,* May 11, 1911.

52. Thomas S. Adams to Haugen, April 1, 1910, Haugen Papers; Adams, "Memorandum on the Income Tax," undated copy in the Haugen papers. (Internal analysis indicates that this very definitely was a commentary on the bill reported by the Joint Committee in January, 1911.)

Tax Commissioner Haugen also supported the manufacturers briefly in 1911, but only in a narrowly self-serving effort to scuttle the bill of Charles McCarthy and Delos O. Kinsman, who had assumed the intellectual leadership of the income tax movement in Wisconsin. Brownlee, "Progressivism and Economic Growth," pp. 229–249.

53. Thomas S. Adams, "The Place of the Income Tax in the Reform of State Taxation," American Economic Association, *Papers and Proceedings,* I (April, 1911), pp. 303, 305, 321.

54. Of course, during that pinnacle year of national progressive enthusiasm, 1912, Charles McCarthy advanced the proposition that Wisconsin had become a social laboratory whose innumerable experiments, including the adoption of income taxation, were worthy of widespread imitation. But there is no indication that in 1911 McCarthy believed either that other

states would emulate Wisconsin's tax reform or, more significantly, that such emulation should affect an evaluation of the impact of Wisconsin's own tax. McCarthy, *The Wisconsin Idea* (New York, 1912).

55. Bill proposed by Special Joint Committee, April 28, 1911, copy in files of WLRL. The bill is to be distinguished from the slightly different measure introduced as 573, S, on May 19, 1911, and subsequently enacted into law after some revision.

56. The ratios between local assessed valuations and the full-value state assessments were consistently higher for farmers' personal property than for manufacturers' personal property. State of Wisconsin, Tax Commission, *Report,* 1911, 106.

57. *Milwaukee Sentinel,* May 11, 1911.

58. *Milwaukee Sentinel,* June 10, 1911; *The Evening Wisconsin,* June 29, 1911.

59. *The Evening Wisconsin,* June 23, 1911; *Milwaukee Free-Press,* June 24 and June 30, 1911; *Madison Democrat,* June 24, 1911; *Milwaukee Daily News,* June 24, 1911.

60. *Milwaukee Free-Press,* June 15, 1911; see also n. 51, this chapter.

61. See statement of George D. Bartlett, Secretary of Wisconsin Bankers' Association, *Milwaukee Sentinel,* Feb. 5, 1911. Personal property was measured by the value of the bank stock held by investors. When, in 1927, the state again applied the income tax to banks it was considered a form of "tax relief." State of Wisconsin, Tax Commission, *Report,* 1930, pp. 38–43.

62. Memorandum, dated 1912, in Harry W. Bolens Papers; *Milwaukee Sentinel,* May 26, 1911.

63. Otto Falk to Bolens, June 2, 1911, Bolens Papers; F. G. Simmons to Francis E. McGovern, June 8, 1911, Francis E. McGovern Papers, SHSW. "Genesis of Wisconsin's Income Tax Law, an Interview with D. O. Kinsman," *Wisconsin Magazine of History,* XXI (Sept. 1937), p. 12; *The Evening Wisconsin,* June 29, 1911; *Milwaukee Daily News,* June 29, 1911.

64. Bill 573, S, as introduced on May 19, 1911, McCarthy Papers. See John F. Sinclair to Kinsman, June 6, 1911, files of WLRL, for summary of changes made in original McCarthy-Kinsman bill; State of Wisconsin, Tax Commission, *The Wisconsin Income Tax Law* (Madison, 1911). Also, the income tax act exempted "intangibles" and farm machinery and implements from personal property taxation.

65. *Milwaukee Sentinel,* June 10, 1911.

In the first year of the income tax only about 3% of those individuals who paid an income tax in 12 representative counties were farmers. In those counties, of the farmers who were assessed an income tax, almost three fourths paid no tax because of the personal property offset, as contrasted with only 30% for all individuals assessed an income tax. Wisconsin Tax Commission, *Report*, 1912, pp. 34 and 38. Further, this very poor performance of the income tax within agricultural communities may well confirm the traditional urban suspicions that farmers would be able to avoid the tax by obscuring their true net incomes. See, for example, Charles Bullock, "The State Income Tax and Classified Property Tax," *Proceedings of the National Tax Association,* Vol. 10 (1916), p. 378.

Chapter 4

1. For an account of the success of the Wisconsin railroads in turning progressive regulatory legislation to their benefit, see Stanley Caine, *The Myth of a Progressive Reform: Railroad Regulation in Wisconsin, 1903–1910* (Madison, 1970), and "Why Railroads Supported Regulation: The Case of Wisconsin, 1905–1910," *Business History Review,* XLIV (Summer, 1970), pp. 175–189.

2. To investigate the application of the penalty rate and the full set of Tax Commission policies, including those discussed hereafter, an examination was made of the returns of all the manufacturing corporations that had earned a taxable income of $500,000 or more in any one of the years 1913, 1916, 1919, 1922, 1925, and 1928 (as determined from the income tax rolls). There were 64 such corporations and for 52 of them full sets of income tax returns were extant. For these firms, the Tax Commission made 13 additional assessments over the period of our study. Of these, three involved the application of the penalty rate. See Note on Sources.

3. In fact, it was not until 1915 that a governor appointed a Tax Commissioner from Milwaukee, and at no time during our period did a governor make an appointment from Racine-Kenosha or the Fox River Valley cities. The only Commissioner trained as an economist was T. S. Adams, who served from 1911 to 1915.

4. *Evening Wisconsin,* May 24, 1912; *Milwaukee Sentinel,* May 26 and May 28, 1912; *Milwaukee Free-Press,* June 1, 1912; *Milwaukee Sentinel,* June 3, 1912. A Wisconsin Supreme Court ruling upheld this principle. *State of Wisconsin ex rel. Gisholt Machine Co. v. Norsman,* 168 Wis. 422.

5. For a discussion of the administration of the income tax, with full citation of sources, see W. Elliot Brownlee, "Progressivism and Economic Growth," pp. 103–135.

6. A summary of the income tax ideas Bolens used in his 1912 speeches is found in the Bolens Papers, State Historical Society of Wisconsin (SHSW). See, also, *Milwaukee Journal,*

Aug. 12, 1912; *Milwaukee Daily News,* Aug. 28, 1912; *Milwaukee Sentinel,* Nov. 1, 1912.

7. McGovern, despite his political origins in the Milwaukee urban reform movement of the 1890's and some consequent personal doubts about the income tax, was beholden for electoral support primarily to the traditional progressive sources, the agricultural and small town populations, and never wavered in his support of the tax. Indeed, McGovern's weakest area of statewide support was his Milwaukee home; he never carried the city in either of his gubernatorial campaigns. *Milwaukee Free Press,* June 30, 1912; Jorgen Weibull, "The Wisconsin Progressives, 1900–14," *Mid-America,* 47 (July, 1965), pp. 215 ff.

8. Typescript of speech of Governor Francis E. McGovern, delivered at the West Side Turn Hall, Milwaukee, October 9, 1912, in Bolens Papers, SHSW. For the arguments of Nils Haugen, who led the experts in defending the tax, see *Milwaukee Journal,* Aug. 10, 1912, and a speech, "The Income Tax," Wisconsin Farmers Institute, *Bulletin* (1912), pp. 108–118.

9. See, for example, Charles McCarthy to George W. Perkins, Nov. 23, 1912, in Charles McCarthy Papers, SHSW. On the distribution of McGovern's 1912 vote, weighted toward traditionally progressive rural areas, see Jorgen Weibull, "The Wisconsin Progressives, 1900–14," pp. 218 ff.

10. My discussion of Philipp relies heavily on the biography of Philipp by Robert S. Maxwell which, while very sound, contains little on the connections between Philipp's business interests, the interests of the manufacturing community, and Philipp's politics. See Maxwell, *Emanuel L. Philipp, Wisconsin Stalwart* (Madison, 1959), especially pp. 18–29 on Philipp's business career and pp. 58–59 on Philipp's political life through 1914. Also useful is Herbert Margulies, "The Decline of Wisconsin Progressivism, 1911–1914," *Mid-America,* XXVIII (July, 1957), pp. 146–155.

11. Emanuel L. Philipp, *The Truth About Wisconsin Freight Rates, Views of the Shippers and the Press* (1904); Raymond V. Phelan, *The Financial History of Wisconsin* (Madison, 1908), p. 197. See, also, Stanley P. Caine, *The Myth of a Progressive Reform,* pp. 30–37. (Caine, however, does not treat the division of interest in railroad regulation among manufacturers.)

12. It is true that Philipp probably owed his victory in 1914 in part to voter reaction to higher taxes, as several historians have suggested. Nonetheless, that reaction was not to the income tax, but rather to the abnormally high state property tax levied in 1913. The income tax contributed to this only indirectly in that in 1912 the McGovern administration had become so enthusiastic about the revenue potential of the income tax that it remitted an excessively large portion of state property taxes. The consequent revenue pinch in 1913, exacerbated by new state obligations for

county aid covering highway finance, necessitated an unusually high property tax levy. Subsequently, Philipp campaigned on the issues of extravagance and high property taxes, supported by La Follette's criticism of the McGovern administration. The property tax episode, in fact, increased farmer enthusiasm for the income tax, which only a very small percentage had to pay. Wisconsin Tax Commission, "Taxes of the State of Wisconsin and Its Political Subdivisions, 1901–1936," pp. 11–13; *La Follette's Magazine,* July 25, 1914; Brownlee, "Progressivism and Economic Growth," pp. 267–268; Herbert F. Margulies, *The Decline of the Progressive Movement in Wisconsin, 1890–1910* (Madison, 1968), pp. 142–163; Maxwell, *Emanuel L. Philipp,* pp. 72–89.

13. "In the Matter of Investigation Provided for by Joint Resolution 11 A," typescript of hearings, March 16–April 20, 1915, in files of the Wisconsin Legislative Reference Library, (WLRL); *Milwaukee Sentinel,* June 14 and June 24, 1915; *Milwaukee Journal,* June 22 and June 25, 1915; Charles D. Rosa's memorandum on the 1918 special session of the legislature, undated in Charles D. Rosa Papers; "Wisconsin Bills Imposing or Affecting Surtaxes on Income Which Were Not Enacted, 1911–1955," Informational Bulletin No. 145, Oct. 1955, files of WLRL; "Changes in Assessment and Tax Laws in Wisconsin Made by Legislature in 1919," memorandum in Haugen Papers, SHSW; Merle Curti and Vernon Carstensen, *The University of Wisconsin,* II (Madison, 1949), pp. 207–213; Margulies, *The Decline of the Progressive Movement in Wisconsin,* pp. 239–242; Maxwell, *Emanuel L. Philipp,* pp. 155 ff.; State of Wisconsin, *Journal of the Senate,* June 4, 1920, pp. 61–64; State of Wisconsin, Tax Commission, *Wisconsin Income Tax Law,* 1919, pp. 56–62.

14. For an analysis of these initiatives and the more general process of institutional adaptation on the part of Wisconsin's farmers to the industrial revolution, see Eric E. Lampard, *The Rise of the Dairy Industry in Wisconsin, A Study in Agricultural Change, 1820–1920* (Madison, 1963). For a discussion of parallel developments in Iowa, see Keach Johnson, "Iowa Dairying at the Turn of the Century: The New Agriculture and Progressivism," *Agricultural History,* XLV (April, 1971), pp. 95–110.

15. For a discussion of the role of entrepreneurs like William D. Henry in promoting the institutionalization of research and the orderly dissemination of scientific knowledge on behalf of productivity among farmers, see Charles E. Rosenberg, "Science, Technology, and Economic Growth: The Case of the Agricultural Experiment Station Scientist, 1875–1914," *Agricultural History,* XLV (January, 1971), pp. 1–20.

16. Lampard, *The Rise of the Dairy Industry,* pp. 244 ff.; William H. Glover, *Farm and College, The College of Agriculture of the University of Wisconsin* (Madison, 1952), pp. 187–227.

17. Between 1897 and 1901, the Wisconsin Farmers' Institute, the Wisconsin State Grange, the Wisconsin Dairymen's Association, and the Wisconsin State Board of Agriculture all recommended state aids for highway development. The first president of the Good Roads Association, formed in 1907, was William D. Hoard. Ballard Campbell, "The Good Roads Movement in Wisconsin, 1890–1911," *Wisconsin Magazine of History,* XLIX (Summer, 1966), pp. 284 and 288.

18. For a discussion of the earlier cultural backlash from William D. Hoard's 1890 support, as Governor, of the Bennett Law (1889), which imposed compulsory education in English, see Roger E. Wyman, "Wisconsin Ethnic Groups and the Election of 1890," *Wisconsin Magazine of History,* 51 (Summer, 1968), pp. 269–293. Also on the contribution of William D. Hoard and the state's dairy farmers to the formation of new Republican coalition around La Follette during the 1890's, see Robert S. Maxwell, *La Follette and the Rise of the Progressives in Wisconsin* (Madison, 1956), pp. 13 and 62; Lampard, *The Rise of the Dairy Industry,* pp. 341–342; and David P. Thelen, *The New Citizenship, Origins of Progressivism in Wisconsin, 1885–1900* (Columbia, Mo., 1972), pp. 296, 299.

19. State of Wisconsin, Tax Commission, *Report of the Wisconsin Tax Commission* (Madison, 1907), pp. 182–183, 223–224 and 245–246; Tax Commission, *Special Report on The Finances of The State Government* (Madison, 1911), p. 104. These estimates of the dollar size of the agricultural service state are absolute minimums (lower bounds) as a result of the exclusion of state aids for schools and highway and the exclusion of programs whose direct benefits went only partially to farmers. (Such programs included the support of the Commissioners of Fisheries, support of the St. Louis World Fair of 1904, maintenance of the Veterans' Home, and, most significantly, subsidization of the State University, including the Agricultural College.)

20. The extent of overlapping of these reform interests is suggested by the finding of Louis Galambos that during the period 1890–1920, even among the midwestern farm journals which were directed at farmers interested in scientific agriculture, attitudes toward large corporations continued to be considerably more unfavorable than favorable, despite farm prosperity and the gradual improvement in the corporate image. See Louis Galambos, "The Agrarian Image of the Large Corporation, 1879–1920: A Study in Social Accommodation," *The Journal of Economic History,* XXVIII (Sept., 1968), pp. 341–362.

21. State of Wisconsin, Tax Commission, *Second Annual Report on the Statistics of Municipal Finances* (Madison, 1917), pp. 54–57.

22. Such efforts peaked in 1923 with a vigorous campaign of

the Milwaukee Association of Commerce to bring farmer and manufacturer together and, at the same time, to lend farmers the expertise of manufacturers in coping with the marketplace. For example, Emanuel L. Philipp and Lawrence C. Whittet sponsored a "Farmers and Business Men's Conference," featuring themselves, W. H. Alford of Nash Motors, Henry L. Russell of the College of Agriculture, the Wisconsin Commissioner of Agriculture, and the leaders of the Wisconsin Farm Bureau, the Society of Equity, and the Wisconsin Dairymen's Association, to discuss the full range of farm problems, but stressing the development of "farming as a business." See *Bulletin of the Milwaukee Association of Commerce,* July 5 and July 19, 1923. See, also, for example, *Civics and Commerce,* August, 1916, pp. 9–10; October, 1917, pp. 7–8, 18; and November and December, 1917, pp. 6–7.

23. Merle Curti and Vernon Carstensen, *The University of Wisconsin, A History,* Volume II (Madison, 1949), p. 212.

24. In particular, these farmers opposed the effort, intensified during the 1920's, of the more radical progressives to tie the funding of the University to surtaxes rather than the traditional mill taxes on general property. That conflict as to the manner of financing the University during the 1920's reflected a more fundamental rift between farm progressives. As the marketing problems of farmers came to the fore once again during the recession 1914–15, the ideas of the Society of Equity, focusing on crop-withholding, made inroads not only among the state's grain and livestock producers but also among its dairymen. As the center of political gravity moved toward the cooperative movement of the American Farm Bureau as an acceptable alternative to the Society of Equity, the College of Agriculture under Dean Harry L. Russell found itself in the conservative wing of the farmer movement and subject to budgetary attacks as an elitist institution. However, the attachment of even the more radical farmers of northern Wisconsin to the state services, such as the county agent program, remained strong, and the disagreement in no way prevented farm progressives from uniting on the 1925 tax reform package. For a discussion of the budgetary problems of the University, see Merle Curti and Vernon Carstensen, *The University of Wisconsin,* Vol. II, pp. 211 ff. On the clash between Harry L. Russell and farm leaders promoting cooperative marketing, see Edward H. Beardsley, *Harry L. Russell and Agricultural Science in Wisconsin* (Madison, 1969), pp. 92 ff. and 137 ff.

25. It should be noted that little or no evidence exists to suggest that the reliance on income taxation yielded an educational system of unusually high quality. In fact, the reluctance of the state to incur debts, coupled with the provision of farm property relief, restricted the growth of the public education, in comparison with other Great Lakes states. As result, even after

almost a decade in income taxation, in 1920 per-pupil expenditures and average annual teachers salaries, two measures of educational quality, were lower in Wisconsin than in any other Great Lakes state at levels about 90% of the Great Lakes average. Department of Commerce, Bureau of Foreign and Domestic Commerce, *Statistical Abstract of the United States, 1919* (Washington, 1920), pp. 106–107.

Despite the benefits which urban communities received from such state aids, an unusually large portion of tax revenues were returned to county governments, which tended to use the resources gained to finance rural services. This is entirely consistent with the rural base for Wisconsin's highway improvement campaigns. Campbell, "The Good Roads Movement in Wisconsin, 1890–1911," pp. 278–293.

26. More than one third of the large growth in state tax revenues between 1925 and 1930, from $28.4 million to $47.4 million, went to increase state aids. Almost all of the increase in state revenues was accounted for by increases in motor vehicle taxes and income taxes. While other categories of taxes declined in relative importance, the share of state taxes accounted for by income taxes more than doubled and that accounted for by motor vehicle taxes increased about 50%. (See Table.)

Composition of State Taxes

	Fiscal 1925	Fiscal 1930
General property taxes	17%	9%
Special property taxes	27	17
Other special taxes	7	6
Inheritance taxes	11	5
Income tax	8	21
Motor vehicle tax	30	42
Total	100	100

SOURCE: State of Wisconsin, Tax Commission, *Taxes of the State of Wisconsin and Its Political Subdivisions, 1901–1936, Bulletin No. 76* (August, 1936), 18, 20.

27. Vernon Carstensen, *Farms or Forests: Evolution of a State Land Policy for Northern Wisconsin, 1850–1932* (Madison, 1958); Arlan Helgeson, *Farms in the Cutover: Agricultural Settlement in Wisconsin* (Madison, 1962); Erling D. Solberg, *New Laws for New Forests* (Madison, 1961); Walter A. Rowlands, "The Great Lakes Cutover Region," in Merrill Jensen (ed.), *Regionalism in America* (Madison and Milwaukee, 1965), pp. 331–346; Bushrod W. Allin, "The Cutover Region of the Great Lakes States," in Carter Goodrich (ed.), *Migration and Economic Opportunity* (Philadelphia, 1936), pp. 164–201. See, also, Harley L. Lutz, "The Problem of State Aid, Local Tax Burdens and Tax Delinquency in Wisconsin," November, 1924, copy in files of Herman Ekern, Box #45, SHSW.

28. Herbert F. Margulies, *The Decline of the Progressive*

Movement in Wisconsin, pp. 244–282; Margulies, "The La Follette-Philipp Alliance of 1918," *Wisconsin Magazine of History,* XXVIII (Summer, 1955), pp. 248–249; Margulies, "The Election of 1920 in Wisconsin: The Return to 'Normalcy' Reappraised," *Wisconsin Magazine of History,* XLI (Autumn, 1957), pp. 15–22; Robert S. Maxwell, *Emanuel L. Philipp, Wisconsin Stalwart,* pp. 206–208; Michael P. Rogin, *The Intellectuals and McCarthy: The Radical Specter* (Cambridge, 1967), pp. 72–75; Theodore Saloutos, "The Decline of the Wisconsin Society of Equity," *Agricultural History,* 15 (July, 1941), pp. 137–150.

29. Charles D. Rosa to his supporters in a congressional campaign, September, 1920, in Charles D. Rosa Papers, SHSW.

30. Before devoting himself to the difficult political and economic questions of comprehensive tax reform, Blaine relied on accomplishing the rather meaningless repeal of the secrecy clause protecting income tax returns, supporting the adoption of a teachers' retirement fund surtax Philipp had promoted, and embracing, rather traditionally, effective income tax administration.

31. Charles D. Rosa, "Address before the Joint Committee on Finance of the Senate and Assembly," Feb. 21, 1923, typescript in the Rosa Papers; M. B. Olbrich, quoted in *Wisconsin State Journal,* April 23, 1923.

32. For a discussion of the role of the expert defenders of income taxation during the 1920's, see Brownlee, "Progressivism and Economic Growth," pp. 45–49 and 55–64. On the trends in state taxation, see pp. 42–43 of this book. On concurrent federal tax policy, which included the reduction of the impact of federal taxation on manufacturing, see Randolph E. Paul, *Taxation in the United States* (Boston, 1954), pp. 122–142; Sidney Ratner, *American Taxation, Its History as a Social Force in Democracy* (New York, 1942), pp. 400–433.

33. The protection to farmers was possible because (1) the shrinkage of farm incomes had rendered the offset of little value to farmers and (2) the new income tax revenues would permit the reduction of state property taxes. State of Wisconsin, Tax Commission, *Report,* 1916, pp. 76–80; 1918, pp. 6–8; 1920, pp. 31–43; 1922, pp. 16–19; 1924, pp. 66–77; Herbert D. Simpson, "The Effects of a Property Tax Off-set Under an Income Tax," Institute for Economic Research, *Studies in Public Finance* (Research Monograph No. 3), Richard T. Ely (ed.) (Chicago, 1932); Harley Lutz, "Memorandum on the Revision of the Wisconsin Income Tax," Dec. 15, 1924, in Herman Ekern Papers, SHSW.

34. *Wisconsin Agriculturalist* (Racine), Feb. 3, March 7, April 28, 1923, and Feb. 28, 1925; Charles H. Everett to James J. Blaine, Jan. 22, 1923, James J. Blaine Papers; *Wisconsin Farmer* (Des Moines, Iowa), Feb. 19, Feb. 26, and July 23, 1925; *Wisconsin State Journal,* Jan. 24, May 23, 1923, March 10, July 15,

and July 23, 1925; *Capital Times,* Feb. 21, March 12, July 9, July 22, and July 23, 1925; *Milwaukee Journal,* Jan. 23, 1923, Feb. 28, March 15, and July 26, 1925; *Milwaukee Sentinel,* Jan. 23, Jan. 25, March 6, March 7, and May 5, 1923; Charles D. Rosa. "Special Session, 1922," undated memorandum, Rosa Papers, SHSW; Rosa to George Bubar, March 11, 1923, Rosa Papers; A. J. Myrland to Nils P. Haugen, Feb. 1, 1923, Haugen Papers, SHSW.

35. *Milwaukee Sentinel,* Feb. 21, March 1, March 8, and May 5, 1923; Testimony of Louis Arnold (Milwaukee's Socialist Tax Commissioner), Minutes of the Joint Committee on Finance, Meeting No. 19, Feb. 21, 1923, typescript in files of WLRL; *Milwaukee Journal,* March 8, 1923; *Wisconsin State Journal,* May 23, 1923.

36. W. Elliot Brownlee, "Progressivism and Economic Growth," pp. 281 ff.

37. Maxwell, *Emanuel L. Philipp, Wisconsin Stalwart,* pp. 215–217; Bayrd Still, *Milwaukee, The History of a City* (Madison, 1948), pp. 508–509; *Civics and Commerce,* 1911–1921; *Milwaukee,* 1921–1923; *Bulletin of the Milwaukee Association of Commerce,* 1923–29; Wisconsin Manufacturers' Association, *Industrial Wisconsin,* December, 1916, copy in Fred H. Clausen Papers, SHSW.

38. Philipp to Arthur J. Dodge, March 28, 1923, Emanuel L. Philipp Papers, SHSW; *Milwaukee Journal,* January 24, 1923; Edmond C. Breese to members of the Milwaukee Association of Commerce, April 27, 1923, Philipp Papers; Lawrence C. Whittet to John M. Whitehead, April 26, 1923, in John M. Whitehead Papers, SHSW.

39. For a survey of the recruiting effort by the MAC, see H. B. Mortimer to Philipp, June 3, 1924, Philipp Papers. See also Lawrence C. Whittet to Richard H. Edmonds, August 20, 1924, Philipp Papers. In addition to favoring the negative approach of the WMA and the prior commitment to their effort, some manufacturers apparently disliked the strong attachment to the Greater Wisconsin Association to Milwaukee interests. Phil Grau to A. D. Bolens, Nov. 12, 1928, in A. D. Bolens Papers, SHSW.

40. The Anti-Saloon League actually had a manufacturers' committee. Herbert Margulies, *The Decline of the Progressive Movement in Wisconsin,* p. 266.

41. A compromise in 1923 favoring the manufacturers might have included some combination of a partial offset retention, a lower corporate rate, and a more modest change in the distribution formula. Edmund C. Breese to members of the Milwaukee Association of Commerce, April 27, 1923, Emanuel E. Philipp Papers, SHSW; A. J. Myrland, Secretary of the Wisconsin Tax Commission, to Nils P. Haugen, Feb. 2, 1923, Haugen Papers; *Milwaukee Sentinel,* Feb. 22 and March 30, 1923. One manufacturer, furniture-maker William Mauthe of Fond du Lac, did contribute to

the pressures brought to bear upon the anti-Blaine progressive W. A. Titus to vote against the final compromise, which failed to pass in 1923. But Mauthe was one of the extremely rare manufacturers who was a La Follette supporter himself, and his activities in 1923 were not related directly to those of the important manufacturers. It is suggestive of the rigidity of Wisconsin manufacturers that even Mauthe, with his progressive ties, was opposed to compromise efforts. *The Milwaukee Sentinel,* June 22, 1923; *The Capital Times,* June 22, 1923; William Mauthe to Blaine, June 19, 1923, Mauthe to Robert M. La Follette, Jr., June 19, 1923, Blaine to Mauthe, June 20, 1923, Mauthe to Blaine, June 21, 1923, Mauthe to Blaine, June 23, 1923, Mauthe to Blaine, June 26, 1923, Blaine to Mauthe, June 20, 1923, Blaine Papers.

42. Indicative of the weakening of the manufacturers' support among legislators was the fact that William Mauthe continued, in 1925, to oppose reform without posing alternative programs; but this time he was unable to exert any leverage on the proceedings. *The Milwaukee Sentinel,* Feb. 21 and March 24, 1925; Mauthe to William T. Evjue, March 4, 1925 and Mauthe to Blaine, April 21, 1925, Blaine Papers.

43. Edwin E. Witte, "Chronology of the Activities of The Wisconsin Manufacturers' Association to Defeat Increases in Income Taxes," memorandum prepared at the request of Governor Blaine, March 2, 1925, Edwin E. Witte Papers, SHSW.

44. National Industrial Conference Board, *The Tax Problem in Wisconsin* (New York, 1924). For an analysis of this report, see Brownlee, "Progressivism and Economic Growth," pp. 49 ff.

45. W. A. Freehof, "Wisconsin Industry Rebels at Income Tax," in *The Annalist* (New York), Dec. 25, 1925, and Henry Schott, "It's a Family Argument in Wisconsin," *Nation's Business* (Washington, D.C.), August, 1925. Also, see Michigan Manufacturers' *Financial Record,* October 25, 1924, and *Chicago Tribune,* February 28, 1925.

46. The manufacturers hoped to be able to deduct contributions to the WMA from their taxable income. Perusal of the correspondence within the restricted income tax return files reveals that this question was a constant source of irritation between the Tax Commission and the manufacturers, with the Tax Commission ruling uniformly that deductions to that association were not allowable as they did not serve an "educational" purpose. Also, see Franklin D. Strader (under the signature of A. J. Myrland) to A. F. North (Field Auditor for Tax Commission), May 17, 1922, in A. F. North Papers, Wisconsin State Archives.

47. For a brief summary of business interest in public relations, especially in the 1920's, see Thomas C. Cochran, *The American Business System, A Historical Perspective, 1900–1955* (Cambridge, 1965), pp. 76–78, and for an extensive description

of public relations entrepreneurs, see Alan R. Raucher, *Public Relations and Business, 1900–1929* (Baltimore, 1968).

48. W. H. Alford to Albert D. Bolens, March 28, 1925, A. D. Bolens Papers, SHSW.

49. These manufacturers included Carl A. Johnson, president of Gisholt Machine Co., Walter Kohler, president of Kohler Co., George Vits, president of the Aluminum Goods Manufacturing Co., W. H. Alford, vice-president of Nash Motors Co., Otto H. Falk, president of Allis Chalmers Co., and F. H. Clausen, president of Van Brunt Manufacturing Co.

50. Walter J. Kohler to Bolens, Dec. 11, 1924, A. D. Bolens Papers, SHSW.

51. Other conservatives, particularly overly zealous newspaper editors, did occasionally argue that the consumer and the laborer would pay for increases in income taxation. But the use of such arguments was definitely rare. For examples of the exceptions, see editorials in *Milwaukee Journal,* Jan. 23, 1923, and *Wisconsin Agriculturalist,* Feb. 28, 1925.

52. A complete set of the advertisements may be found in the files of the WLRL.

53. Contributing to the increasingly progressive cast of the issues was the massive and swift response to the Gottlieb Conference Board Report and the WMA advertisements by Wisconsin tax experts, including Edwin E. Witte, John R. Commons, and Harley L. Lutz. Uniformly, they denounced the manufacturers' statements as nothing more than special pleading. Brownlee, "Progressivism and Economic Growth," pp. 55–63.

54. For the reiteration of the manufacturers' position in 1925, stated mainly by Frederick H. Clausen, then president of the WMA, see *Milwaukee Journal,* Feb. 10, Feb. 18, and March 17, 1925; *Milwaukee Sentinel,* Feb. 14, Feb. 28, March 13, and April 15, 1925; *Wisconsin State Journal,* Feb. 17, 1925; *Capital Times,* Feb. 17 and Feb. 18, 1925. The general position of the manufacturers had hardened to the extent that when Burt Williams, a tax consultant with business ties, tried to organize a propaganda movement to emphasize Wisconsin's economic virtues, he found manufacturers far less amenable to a positive campaign than had been the case in 1923. Albert D. Bolens, pro-business newspaper publisher and editor whose views coincided with those of the WMA, characterized Williams' proposed line of argument as "apologetic piffle" that would serve only to "encourage the Madison administration to continue its harmful course." *Port Washington Star,* June 12, 1925.

55. Alford to A. D. Bolens, March 28, 1925; F. H. Clausen to Bolens, March 28, 1925, A. D. Bolens Papers.

56. Among the proponents of more radical tax measures were Herman J. Severson of Waupaca County, Speaker of the Assembly, John L. Dahl of Rice Lake, and Tax Commissioner Charles Rosa, all of whom Blaine had neglected in framing tax legislation. He concentrated on refuting the claims of Attorney General Herman Ekern that he had made a major contribution to reducing the burden of property taxation on Wisconsin's farmers. Rosa, quite correctly, pointed out that assessed values of farm property had been falling from the onset of the postwar depression and that the direction of the Tax Commission played the major role in facilitating that process.

After the primary in which Zimmerman defeated Ekern, Rosa even withdrew from the Tax Commission to run for the Senate, not with any hope of winning but hoping to draw off progressive votes from Blaine to throw the election to Irvine L. Lenroot, despite his more conservative posture. Rosa was unsuccessful, and Zimmerman reappointed him to the Commission. See correspondence of Charles Rosa, March-September, 1926, Rosa Papers, SHSW.

57. William J. Campbell, "History of the Republican Party Under Convention Plan, 1924 to 1940," in William J. Campbell Papers, SHSW; William J. Campbell to A. D. Bolens, August 12, September 20, October 4, November 22, and November 24, 1926 and Bolens to Campbell, November 23, 1926; Alford to Bolens, June 28, 1927, in A. D. Bolens Papers, SHSW. Campbell was the leader of the Oshkosh Republicans whom the manufacturers bypassed in 1926.

58. The suggestions of the manufacturers included deduction of only 5% of personal property from taxable income, a reduction of the corporate rate to 4%, and an increase of the city's share of income tax revenues to 65%, rather than the 70% advocated by the Socialists. Wisconsin Manufacturers' Association, "A Tax Plan for Wisconsin," undated pamphlet, files of WLRL; *Milwaukee Journal,* April 19, 1926.

59. Farm progressives succeeded in increasing the appropriation for auditing income tax returns, enhancing the power of the Tax Commission in collecting delinquent taxes, and permitted municipalities to employ experts to aid in property assessments.

The conservative and urban progressive proposals that failed included full exemption of personal property from taxation, repeal of the teachers' retirement surtax, restoration of the personal property tax offset, and reinstitution of the pre-1925 distribution formula. The latter was championed by Milwaukee's Socialist Mayor, Daniel W. Hoan, and the League of Wisconsin Municipalities. Hoan criticized the suspension of the state property tax that Blaine had engineered after passage of the 1925 reforms as accomplished by a "steal" of twenty million dollars out of the city treasuries. Hoan was correct in that one effect of the 1925 reforms was to extend a tax break to general property at the expense of incomes, thereby removing resources from the taxing ambit of localities. In 1926, for example, only 69% of the state's general property was located in "urban" places ("cities" and "villages"), as compared with 94% of taxable income (using assessed income taxes as an approximation) having an "urban" origin. State of Wisconsin, Tax Commission, *Report,* 1926, pp. 12 and 243.

Edwin E. Witte, "Bills in the 1927 Session Indicating the Position Taken by the La Follette Progressives," Edwin E. Witte Papers, SHSW; WMA, "A Tax Plan for Wisconsin," p. 2; *Milwaukee Journal,* Dec. 12, 1926, Feb. 2, Feb. 10, Feb. 11, March 3, March 21, May 5, and May 12, 1927; *Milwaukee Sentinel,* Feb. 16, 1927; *Capital Times,* March 18, May 11, and June 22, 1927; *Wisconsin State Journal,* March 31, 1927; *Daily Northwestern* (Oshkosh), March 13 and May 6, 1927.

60. State of Wisconsin, *Wisconsin Statutes,* 1927; State of Wisconsin, Tax Commission, *Taxes of the State of Wisconsin* (1936), pp. 19–20; Rosa to Brown Katzenbach, April 18, 1927, Fred R. Zimmerman to Wisconsin Tax Commission, July 2, 1928, Wisconsin Tax Commission to Zimmerman, July 25, 1928, Rosa Papers; *Milwaukee Journal,* Sept. 25, Oct. 23, 1927, and June 5, 1928; *Milwaukee Sentinel,* Oct. 22, 1927; *Superior Evening Telegram,* Oct. 22, 1927; *Capital Times,* Oct. 25, 1927, July 7, July 14, July 27, and August 21, 1928; *Wisconsin State Journal,* Oct. 26, Oct. 27, 1927, and July 26, 1928.

On the earlier and later development of the career of Walter J. Kohler, Sr., and the Kohler Company, see Trudi J. Eblen, "A History of the Kohler Company of Kohler, Wisconsin, 1870–1914" (unpublished M.S. thesis, University of Wisconsin, 1965), and Walter H. Uphoff, *Kohler on Strike: Thirty Years of Conflict* (Boston, 1966).

61. A. D. Bolens to L. J. Mahoney, Jan. 14, 1928, and Mrs. Harry E. Thomas to Bolens, Jan. 17, 1930, in A. D. Bolens Papers; William J. Campbell, "History of the Republican Party in Wisconsin . . ." Campbell Papers; State of Wisconsin, *Journal of the Senate,* Sept. 20, 1929, pp. 2133–2142; *Capital Times,* March 22, July 11, July 16, and Aug. 30, 1929; *Wisconsin State Journal,* April 28, July 22, August 30, and Sept. 18, 1929; *Milwaukee Journal,* July 12, July 24, and Sept. 17, 1929.

Chapter 5

1. A sensitive examination of the interrelationship between the mass-movement and interest-group character of Wisconsin progressivism, but one with a different assessment of the relative

roles of agricultural forces and, perhaps implicitly, the manufacturers, is David P. Thelen, "Robert La Follette's Leadership, 1891–96, The Old and New Politics and the Dilemma of the Progressive Politician," *Pacific Northwest Quarterly,* 62 (July, 1971), pp. 97–108.

2. On the disposition of manufacturers toward this legislation, see the survey of manufacturer opinion conducted by the Wisconsin Manufacturers Association at the request of the U.S. Commission on Industrial Relations: "Preliminary Report of Alexander M. Daly, Special Investigator, U.S. Commission on Industrial Relations, Dec., 1914," in Charles McCarthy Papers, State Historical Society of Wisconsin (SHSW).

It is plausible to surmise that the progressive labor legislation very likely had no significant negative impact on economic growth in Wisconsin. Manufacturers clearly benefited from accident insurance eliminating costly common-law accident litigation and very likely found that labor legislation tended to provide them with a higher quality, more stable, more productive labor force.

3. For surveys of Wisconsin's progressive labor enactments in 1911 see Thomas W. Gavett, *Development of the Labor Movement in Milwaukee* (Madison, 1965), pp. 106–111, and Robert S. Maxwell, *La Follette and the Rise of the Progressives in Wisconsin* (Madison, 1956), pp. 153–172.

4. For the history of unemployment insurance legislation in Wisconsin, including a consideration of the crucial role played by farmers, see Daniel Nelson, *Unemployment Insurance, The American Experience, 1915–1935* (Madison, 1969), pp. 104–128.

5. For criticisms of the administration of the Industrial Commission, see Arthur J. Altmeyer, *The Industrial Commission of Wisconsin* (Madison, 1932). The cost of the Industrial Commission, including the Board of Arbitration and the Bureau of Labor, was, in aggregate, consistently rather slight. Even before the relative decline of the Commission in the 1920's, its cost was substantially less than 1% of state-level disbursements. State of Wisconsin, Tax Commission, *Second Annual Report on the Statistics of Municipal Finance* (1917), pp. 54–55.

6. This is not to suggest, as Gabriel Kolko does, that federal progressive legislation tended to spring from a conspiracy of large corporate interests. Although manufacturers at the federal level more easily softened anticorporatism, a significant source of support for extension of the income tax during Woodrow Wilson's administration was rural progressivism. Kolko, *The Triumph of Conservatism* (Chicago, 1967).

7. See Richard M. Abrams, *Conservatism in a Progressive Era: Massachusetts Politics, 1900–1912* (Cambridge, 1964), pp. 1–24.

8. For additional suggestions of this, see Thomas C. Cochran, *The Pabst Brewing Company: The History of an American Business* (New York, 1948), especially Chapter Ten, and Bayrd Still, *Milwaukee, The History of a City* (Madison, 1948), Chapter Thirteen; Thomas W. Gavett, *Development of the Labor Movement in Milwaukee* (Madison, 1965), pp. 114–125. The paternalistic exceptions to this pattern, such as Allis-Chalmers, International Harvester, Bucyrus-Erie, and the Kohler Co., have been overly visible in the historical literature. See Trudi J. Eblen, "A History of the Kohler Company of Kohler, Wisconsin, 1870–1914," unpublished M.S. thesis, University of Wisconsin, 1965; Gerd Korman, *Industrialization, Immigrants and Americanizers* (Madison, 1967); and Harold F. Williamson and Kenneth H. Myers, *Designed for Digging, the First 75 Years of Bucyrus-Erie Company* (Evansville, 1955), especially pp. 127–132.

9. For suggestions of the characteristic western attitudes toward manufacturing in the nineteenth century, see Harvey S. Perloff *et al., Regions, Resources and Economic Growth* (Baltimore, 1960), p. 117, n. 17, and Eric E. Lampard, *The Rise of the Dairy Industry in Wisconsin* (Madison, 1963), pp. 335–336.

10. For a suggestion of the significance of home ownership to Wisconsin manufacturing corporations during the 1920's, see Altmeyer, *The Industrial Commission of Wisconsin*, pp. 8–9.

Excluding cities of less than 10,000 in population, which contained most of the dairy-related manufacturing, in 1929 fully 34.8% of value added by manufacturing in Wisconsin originated in cities of less than 50,000. The comparable share for cities between 10,000 and 50,000 in Illinois was 13.5%; in Michigan, 14.4% and in Ohio, 18.1%. U.S. Department of Commerce, Bureau of the Census, *Census of Manufacturers, Reports by States* (Washington, D.C., 1930), pp. 1414, 251, 399, and 562.

Appendix

1. For the development of this procedure, including the pertinent "neoclassical" assumptions, see W. Douglas Morgan and W. Elliot Bronwlee, "The Impact of State and Local Taxation on Industrial Location: A New Measure." *The Quarterly Review of Economics and Business,* forthcoming in 1974. Models based on net-worth maximization have been used recently to study the impact of federal income taxes. See Robert M. Coen, "Effects of Tax Policy on Investment in Manufacturing," *American Economic Review, Papers and Proceedings,* LVIII (May, 1968), pp. 200–211, and the pioneering contributions of Dale W. Jorgenson, especially Robert E. Hall and Dale W. Jorgenson, "Tax Policy and Investment Behavior," *American Economic Review,* LVII (June, 1967), pp. 391–414.

2. For adjustments to account for complicated interactions of federal, state, and local tax systems, see Brownlee and Morgan, "The Impact of State and Local Taxation," *loc. cit.*

3. There is a useful discussion of the comparability of the industry classifications of the *Census of Manufactures* and the *Statistics of Income* in Daniel Creamer *et al., Capital in Manufacturing and Mining, Its Formation and Financing* (Princeton, 1960), pp. 207–17. Using the census industrial classifications for 1929 requires far fewer reconciliations then when one begins with the 1919 categories.

4. United States Treasury Department, *Statistics of Income for 1919* (Washington, D.C., 1922), p. 20.

5. "Relative size" refers to the share of the national total. Value of product was taken from the *Census of Manufactures* and income from the *Statistics of Income.*

6. W. Elliot Brownlee, "Progressivism and Economic Growth: The Wisconsin Income Tax, 1911–1929," pp. 109–112.

7. Personal property taxes that were offset against income did not include taxes paid on almost all machinery. Any machinery attached to a building was considered part of the building and assessed as real property along with the land and building.

8. The reliability of the census capital data has frequently been questioned, but a recent study finds a high degree of conformity between census and *Statistics of Income* capital accounts, at least for 1919. This confirmation makes one more confident of the census data on taxation as well. See Creamer *et al., Capital in Manufacturing and Mining,* pp. 195–205.

9. The ratio of fixed to total assets for 1904 was used to adjust the 1901 asset data, while the average of the 1904 and 1929 ratios was applied to the 1919 data. *Ibid.,* pp. 241–251.

10. This estimate was based on a sample from *Moody's Manual of Industrials. Ibid.,* pp. 197–199.

11. Bureau of the Census, U.S. Department of Commerce, *Historical Statistics of the United States from Colonial Times to the Present* (Washington, D.C., 1960), p. 656.

12. Solomon Fabricant, *Capital Consumption and Adjustment* (New York, 1938), p. 32.

13. Bureau of the Census, *Historical Statistics,* pp. 379, 381, and 422; Creamer *et al.,* p. 334.

14. For a discussion of the use of capital-goods prices in this model, see Dale W. Jorgenson, "Anticipations and Investment Behavior," in James S. Duesenberry (ed.), *The Brookings Quarterly Econometric Model of the United States* (Chicago, 1965), pp. 56–69.

15. No adjustments were made in capital costs to include the

impact of the federal tax system. Consequently our estimates of capital costs for 1919 and 1929 are understated to the extent that federal income taxation increased capital costs, but it is the interstate comparisons that are of primary interest. Given the deductibility of state and local taxes in calculating net income for federal income taxes, the interstate differentials found in the capital costs test would be reduced somewhat. But levels of federal income taxation were low by modern standards. The effective rates of federal income taxation for income earned in 1919 and 1929 by manufacturing corporations were 26.04% and 10.43%, respectively. Thus, for example, in 1919, the revenue advantage from the federal tax to an "average" firm paying a relatively high state tax bill would have been only 26.04% of the difference between its state tax bill and the state tax bill of a firm with the same income before deduction of state taxes that operated in a lower-tax state. In 1929, the relative saving on federal income taxes would have been only 10.43% of the state tax differential. It is quite clear that inclusion of federal income taxes in the capital costs test would not have altered the basic results of the test. Furthermore, the integration of the federal income tax into our estimates might well have served to add an additional degree of uncertainty to our conclusions without making a significant contribution to the issue at hand. For the effective tax rates, see United States Treasury Department, *Statistics of Income for 1919*, p. 9; *1929*, p. 19.

16. State of Wisconsin, Tax Commission, *The Wisconsin Income Tax Law* (Madison, 1911), p. 13; and *Wisconsin Statutes*, 1929, 71.03 (3).

17. State of Wisconsin, Tax Commission, *The Wisconsin Income Tax Law* (Madison, 1917), p. 51; see n. 20 for the group of large corporations.

18. *Ibid.* (1919), p. 70–72.

19. For a rather complete explanation of the Tax Commission guidelines and general depreciation policy at a later date, in 1924, see Henry B. Nelson, *The Wisconsin Income Tax Law, Interpretations, Rulings and Court Decisions* (Milwaukee, 1924), pp. 79–105. For an interesting statement of the complex problem of interpreting the "reasonableness" of depreciation allowances by a field auditor, see John H. Moore, "Depreciation and Repairs," Papers at Field Auditors Convention, 1925, in Wisconsin State Archives.

20. This effective rate of taxation of interest may in fact be an understatement, as banks provided an undetermined amount of capital to Wisconsin manufacturers and, between 1913 and 1927, banks were returned to heavier taxation under the general property tax.

21. For this and other purposes we examined all the 64 manufacturing corporations that had earned a taxable income of $500,000 or more in any one of the years 1913, 1916, 1919, 1922, 1925, and 1928, as determined from the income tax rolls. Income tax returns were extant for the 52 of these companies. 34 of those 52 presented adequate data.

22. We have no way of determining the response of corporations with only a minor portion of their manufacturing activity in Wisconsin, and our test may overstate the cost of capital to them. In any case, there were only six of these corporations in our sample of the largest corporations.

23. Corporations also may have been indirectly deterred from bank borrowing by high rates of taxation of bank net worth. See n. 20.

INDEX